JAMAICAN CREOLE
TENSES

I'HESHIA HANDY

JAMAICAN
CREOLE
TENSES

ISBN: 979-8-9857370-0-4

Acknowledgements

The author would like to thank family and friends for their support and encouragement of the endeavor to undertake this project. Special thanks to: Shantana Dyer, Camille Green-Wright, Nerissa Noad, Elva Rose, Oshane Sinclair, Byanka White, and Alexia Wright.

Contents

Introduction

When West African people were brought by the British to the West Indies to work as slaves, they spoke many different languages and dialects. Through forced assimilation, people were required to interact with other people who spoke different languages than themselves. This created a need for a common language.

A language emerged from the difficult circumstances of slavery, and this language was Jamaican Creole. It can be thought of as a hybrid language that combines English and West African languages. Words such as *pikni* or *pikini* and *nyam* are often referenced by Jamaicans to be of West African origin. That said, Jamaican Creole has a lot of English or English-sounding words.

While English is the official language of Jamaica, people speak Jamaican Creole with family and friends. In fact, some people speak Jamaican Creole as their first language. Additionally, the language is spoken on a continuum, ranging from what many Jamaicans would regard as 'raw patois' to almost English. In schools and other formal settings, however, people speak standard English. This book compares the grammatical structures of Jamaican Creole and English to help you develop a better understanding of the differences between the languages.

In this book are lessons that will help you to pronounce Jamaican Creole words and compare the formation of Jamaican Creole and English tenses. Jamaican Creole is not a formal language, so there might be a variety of spellings for a particular word when it is written by different people. This book uses the simplest spelling for each syllable of a word to imitate the spoken word as best as possible. The words most commonly used in everyday conversation are used in the examples and exercises included.

It is important to pay attention to the pronunciation key as words may resemble some English words but are not pronounced the same way. They may also not have the same meaning. There are certain words that are pronounced slightly differently in Jamaican Creole than they are in English. These words are included as if they were true Jamaican Creole words. An example of this is the Jamaican Creole word *daag* with English equivalent *dog*.

It is suggested that you use the book *Jamaican Creole Grammar* along with this book to improve your understanding of Jamaican Creole.

Abbreviations Used in This Book

adj.	adjective
adv.	adverb
conj.	conjunction
contr.	contraction
E.	English
JC.	Jamaican Creole
lit.	literally
mod. aux.	modal auxiliary verb
n.	noun
prep.	preposition
pron.	pronoun
v.	verb
v. phrase	verb phrase

Pronunciation of Jamaican Creole Words

The alphabet used in this book is similar to the English alphabet (except the letter û which was added for practical reasons). The letters of both languages generally have the same pronunciations. Unlike in English, however, each letter of the Jamaican Creole alphabet has a set, distinct sound. This means that the letters are always pronounced the same way when used to spell Jamaican Creole words. An example of this is *c*. It is always pronounced with a hard *c* sound in Jamaican Creole, unlike in English where it can take on a *c* or *s* sound. Consider the words *care* and *celebrate*.

Pay careful attention to the pronunciation of each syllable as the word may look like an English word but is pronounced differently in Jamaican Creole. It might also have a different meaning. An example of this is the Jamaican Creole word *dot* (E. *dirt*). It is spelled like the English word *dot* meaning *spot*, but the o is pronounced like the 'o' sound in *dove*. Jamaican Creole diphthongs also have consistent and distinct sounds. A guide to the pronunciation of vowels, consonants, and diphthongs follows with an example of a word imitating the sound. Refer to them as often as necessary.

Vowels

a- sharp *a*, as in *wrap*

e- sharp *e*, as in *bet*

i- sharp *i*, as in *zip*

o- sharp *o*, as in *dove*

u- sharp *u*, as in *put*

û- pronounced like the *i* in *first* and the *u* in *murmur*

Consonants

C is pronounced like English *k*, except before *h*.

Ch is pronounced like the ch in *chicken*.

G is pronounced like the g in *get* before and after vowels. After consonants, it has a softer sound like the g in *hang*.

S is pronounced like the *s* in *sew*.

Consonant combinations are generally used as they are in English, e.g., *ng*, *rt*, *nk*, *nt*, etc. The exception is *ph* where *p* and h have distinct sounds when used in Jamaican Creole. An example of this is *japhan* (a type of informal savings program where people pool their money together and take turns getting lump sum payments). It comes from the English words *drop* and *hand*.

Diphthongs

See the pronunciation of diphthongs below.

> A **diphthong** is a combination of two vowels that is pronounced as a single syllable. The letter *y* is sometimes used in diphthongs, although it is not generally considered a vowel.

aa- pronounced like the long *a* sound in *bath*

ai- pronounced like *ai* in *Taiwan*

au- pronounced like *au* in *augment*

ay- pronounced like *ay* in *aye*

ee- pronounced like *a* in *spray*

ia- pronounced like the *ia* in *Gambia*

ii- pronounced like the *ee* in *queen*

oo- pronounced like the long *o* sound in *float*

ou- pronounced like *ou* in *out*

ua- pronounced like *ua* in *Guatemala*

uo- pronounced *uh-wo*

uu- pronounced like the *oo* sound in *afternoon*

ya- pronounced like the *ya* in *yap*

yaa- pronounced like the *ya* in *kumbaya*

ye- pronounced like the *ye* is *yes*

yu- pronounced like *ew* sound in *nephew* or like *you* in *youth*

Writing Jamaican Creole Sentences

Jamaican Creole uses a lot of English words, and these words are generally pronounced as they are in English. Words that are pronounced slightly differently in Jamaican Creole are spelled with the Jamaican Creole alphabet. An example of this is *ignarant* (E. *ignorant*). Note that words that are indicated to be English (identified with the abbreviation E.) but have an additional meaning when used in Jamaican Creole are pronounced as in English. An example of this is E. *bad*. Jamaicans sometimes use the word *bad* to mean *proficient*.

Using Superscripts To Label Jamaican Creole And English Words

In order to make it easier to read Jamaican Creole sentences, it is suggested that you place *E* superscript above the first letter of English words if the sentence has more Jamaican Creole words, and place *J* superscript above the first letter of Jamaican Creole words if the sentence has more English words. This will make it easier to determine how to pronounce the words in the sentence. For example:

Dem aggo si wa mi a ᴱtalk bout.

In the above sentence, there is only one English word. All other words are in Jamaican Creole. This helps the reader to quickly decide whether to use the Jamaican alphabet or the English alphabet to pronounce each word. It is also less time-consuming to label the least amount of words.

ᴶMi planning to ᴶgoh Nigeria.

In the previous sentence, there are more English words, so we label the Jamaican Creole words.

Equal Number OF Jamaican Creole And English Words

If a sentence has an equal number of Jamaican Creole and English words, label only the words in the language of the first word. For example:

ᴶShi travel often ᴶgoh ᴶa Kingston.
ᴱPaul a mi fren ᴱfrom ᴱschool.

When a sentence has only Jamaican Creole or English words, the words do not need to be labeled with *J* or *E*. For example:

Mi iht lyet inna di iivlin.

John moving to St. Mary.

In the first example, all words are in Jamaican Creole. In the second example, all words are in English.

Using Subscripts To Label Jamaican Creole And English Words

There are certain words that resemble the English words that they came from, and only the last few letters of the words are changed. Some words with the last few letters changed include *further, burger, river,* and *sulfur.*

It is suggested that you write *J* subscript before these last few letters to let the reader know that they should pronounce those letters using the Jamaican Creole alphabet. For example, *further* would become *fur,da*, *burger* would become *burg,a*, *river* would become *riv,a*, and *sulfur* would become *sulf,a*. Also, one could use the Jamaican alphabet to spell the entire word (*fûrda*, *bûrga*, *riva*, and *solfa*), though this can sometimes make it more difficult to determine what English words they came from.

For compound words where the first word is in Jamaican Creole and the second word is in English, it is suggested that you label the English portion of the word with *E* subscript beginning with the first letter. For example, the compound word *handbag* is *han$_E$bag* in Jamaican Creole. If the first word were labeled *E*, then you might mistakenly pronounce the entire word using the English alphabet. When the first word is in English and the second word is in Jamaican Creole, the Jamaican Creole word is labeled with *J* subscript. An example of this is *news,pyepa*.

Jamaican Creole Grammar

Sentences in Jamaican Creole generally have a subject, a verb, and a predicate, and the tenses are usually consistent and simple. Sometimes, verbs are omitted from the sentence, and sentence structure may differ from English structure depending on the type of sentence (such as a statement, command, or question, etc.).

The Parts of a Sentence

Sentences in English and Jamaican Creole generally follow the same structure with subject, verb, and predicate.

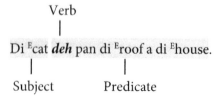

Practice Exercise 1

Look at the following words. Do you recognize these Jamaican Creole words? Try to pronounce them. Also, look at the English translation.

Jamaican Creole	English
aatis	artist
bagabu	caterpillar
chaka-chaka	mess up/untidy
fidem	theirs
gi	give
goh	go
kin oova	tumble over
pudong	put down
seh	say
sidong	sit down

Practice Exercise 2

Write the English translation for the following words.

aggo   _____

bredda   _____

daata   _____

iht   _____

pikini   _____

ruop   _____

soh'mn   _____

sowa   _____

tek   _____

uhman   _____

Practice Exercise 3

Match the following Jamaican Creole words with the English meaning on the right by drawing a line.

aar	sister
cowl	car
daag	supermarket
distraah	tarpaulin
fimmi	her
kyaapet	destroy
kyaar	dog
sista	carpet
supamaakit	cold
trapaalin	mine

Practice Exercise 4

Identify the Jamaican Creole word in the following sentences. Write the word on the line.

1. It is a cloudy dyeh today. _____
2. My madda spends a lot of time planting flowers in her garden. _____
3. The secretary will aada the books for the students tomorrow. _____
4. He placed the glass pan the table. _____
5. It is the fos day of the week. _____
6. The waata settled in the pothole in the middle of the road. _____
7. We are hoping fi the best. _____

8. She was the ong'l student who completed her assignment. _____

9. We can si the blue house on the left side of the road. _____

10. Kerry-Ann sidong at her desk in the classroom. _____

Practice Exercise 5

Write the English word for each Jamaican Creole word you identified in Practice Exercise 4. Write the English word on the line.

1. It is a cloudy dyeh today. _____

2. My madda spends a lot of time planting flowers in her garden. _____

3. The secretary will aada the books for the students tomorrow. _____

4. He placed the glass pan the table. _____

5. It is the fos day of the week. _____

6. The waata settled in the pothole in the middle of the road. _____

7. We are hoping fi the best. _____

8. She was the ong'l student who completed her assignment. _____

9. We can si the blue house on the left side of the road. _____

10. Kerry-Ann sidong at her desk in the classroom. _____

Practice Exercise 6

Write the English translation for the following words on the line. The parts of speech of each word are written to help you determine the English translation.

aweh *adv.* _____   jangcro *n.* _____

datdeh *adj., pron.* _____   nyeli *adv.* _____

faam *n., v.* _____   ong'l *adj., adv.* _____

indeh *contr.* _____   yasso *adv., n.* _____

The Simple Present Tense

The Simple Present Tense of English

In English, the simple present tense of a verb is formed based on the quantity of the subject (singular or plural) as well as the subject it refers to (I, you, she, it etc.). To form the present tense of a regular verb, *s* or *es* is added to the verb of a singular subject. The verb is used in its base infinitive form for plural subjects and the subject *I*.

> The **base infinitive form** of a verb is the form of the verb that is used without adding *to* (an example of this is *run* which differs from the **infinitive form** *to run*).

Look at the formation of the verb *sing* in English:

Person	Subject	Verb Formation
First	I	sing
Second	you	sing
Third	he, she, it	sings
Second (plural)	you	sing
Third (plural)	they, we	sing

As you can see in the previous table, although *I* is singular, it takes the same form as the plural subjects *you*, *they*, and *we*. The verb formation, therefore, depends on both quantity and subject.

The Simple Present Tense of Jamaican Creole

In the simple present tense of Jamaican Creole, verbs are not changed from their base infinitive form. In other words, the same base infinitive form of the verb is used for all subjects of the verb, whether singular or plural. An exception to this is the verb *bi* (which will be discussed in the next lesson).

Look at the formation of the verb *sing* in the Jamaican Creole simple present tense:

Person	Subject	Verb Formation
First	mi	sing
Second	yuh	sing
Third	im, shi, ih	sing
Second (plural)	unnu	sing
Third (plural)	dem, wi	sing

Here are some examples of Jamaican Creole sentences with their English meaning:

Jamaican Creole	English
Mi <u>sing</u> well.	I <u>sing</u> well.
Iih <u>sing</u> well tuh.	He <u>sings</u> well too.
All a wi <u>sing</u> well.	All of us <u>sing</u> well.
Dem <u>sing</u> wid wi.	They <u>sing</u> with us.

In the previous examples, the verb *sing* remains unchanged in its base infinitive form whether the subject is singular or plural. Once the subject has been mentioned, it is easily understood who is *singing*.

Practice Exercise 7

Now that you have learned to form verbs in the simple present tense, translate the following sentences to English.

1. ᴶIm like Serena.

   _____

2. ᴶMi ᴶanti dress well.

   _____

3. ᴱMarsha-Lee uon wau ᴱnice kyaar.

   _____

4. Ricky ᴶsi Misha every ᴶdyeh.

   _____

5. Dem ᴱpresent ih ᴱto di tiicha.

   _____

6. ᴶDi mango fall from ᴶdi tree.

   _____

7. Di ᴱgirl dem goh a di paak.

   _____

8. Di ᴱegret ᴱfly oova di riva.

   _____

9. ᴶWi speak Spanish.

   _____

10. Mi madda wok a di ᴱhospital.

    _____

Practice Exercise 8

Translate the following simple sentences to English.

1. Di pikini [E]like di tyes a [E]ice [E]cream.

   _____

2. [E]Peter-Gaye goh a di gyem wid aar bredda.

   _____

3. [J]Shi always run [J]wau mile [J]pau Sunday.

   _____

4. Mi granmadda [E]love aar granpikini.

   _____

5. Di daag [E]run afta di [E]cat.

   _____

6. Mi likk'l sista [E]jump pan di [E]bed.

   _____

7. Shi ha nof [E]money inna aar [E]bank [E]account.

   _____

8. Iih duh [E]well inna im [E]English tes.

   _____

9. Maas [E]Joe [E]plant [E]yam inna di grong.

   _____

10. [E]Sheila an aar fren [E]study inna di laibri.

   _____

Practice Exercise 9

Use the verbs in brackets to complete the following sentences in the simple present tense. Some verbs are in Jamaican Creole and some are in English. Translate the Jamaican Creole verbs to English and complete each sentence with the correct form of the English verb.

1. We _____ with them each day. (iht)
2. The man _____ callaloo in the market. (sell)
3. They only _____ cash at the school canteen. (tek)
4. Devon _____ very happy at his job. (feel)
5. The company _____ on a fair every year for all the employees. (put)
6. Twelve boys _____ in the detention room. (sidong)
7. We _____ the mountains ahead in the distance. (si)
8. We _____ our mail at the post office once per month. (callek)
9. I _____ the blue car, but it is very old. (like)
10. It _____ sunny outside. (look)

Practice Exercise 10

Identify the Jamaican Creole word in the following sentences. Write the word on the line.

1. Keisha is the bes footballer on the team. _____
2. We live on the adda side of town. _____
3. Trina an Josephine go to the same school, but they live in different cities. _____
4. I hope seh I get something nice for my birthday. _____
5. Im expects his bother at any moment now. _____

6. The bird sits next to the flowa pot on the wall. _____

7. Angie sits on her veranda every morning and sips tea from wau large cup. _____

8. The students fly a Toronto every year. _____

9. Jason takes lunch to school every dyeh. _____

10. Whenever ih rains, water fills the drains. _____

Practice Exercise 11

Write the English word for each Jamaican Creole word you identified in Exercise 10. Write the word on the line.

1. Keisha is the bes footballer on the team. _____

2. We live on the adda side of town. _____

3. Trina an Josephine go to the same school, but they live in different cities. _____

4. I hope seh I get something nice for my birthday. _____

5. Im expects his bother at any moment now. _____

6. The bird sits next to the flowa pot on the wall. _____

7. Angie sits on her veranda every morning and sips tea from wau large cup. _____

8. The students fly a Toronto every year. _____

9. Jason takes lunch to school every dyeh. _____

10. Whenever ih rains, water fills the drains. _____

Practice Exercise 12

Use the following words to form sentences in the simple present tense of Jamaican Creole. Identify the part of speech of the word you used by writing it on the line (e.g. noun, verb, etc.).

anansi *n.* spider

baal *adj., n., v.* bald; cry; shave

kech *n., v.* catch; reach

mash *v.* shatter; to step on

quiz *n., v.* squeeze

san *n., v.* sand

tek *adj., n., v.* take; witty (slang)

1. _____

    Part of speech _____

2. _____

    Part of speech _____

3. _____

    Part of speech _____

4. _____

    Part of speech _____

5. _____

    Part of speech _____

6. _____

    Part of speech _____

7. _____

    Part of speech _____

Present Formation of the Verb Bi

The English Verb Be

The English verb *be* is irregular in the present tense. If you look at the formation of *be* below, you will see that its formation differs from that of a regular verb.

> **Irregular verbs** have formations that do not follow the pattern of regular verbs (that is, adding *s* or es to the verb of a singular subject and using the verb in its base infinitive form for a plural subject and the subject *I*).

The following table outlines the formation of the verb *be* in the English present tense:

Person	Subject	Verb Formation
First	I	am
Second	you	are
Third	he, she, it	is
Second (plural)	you	are
Third (plural)	they, we	are

The Jamaican Creole Verb Bi

The Jamaican Creole verb *bi* (E. be) is also irregular in the simple present tense of Jamaican Creole. Its formation is *a*.

The following table outlines the formation of the verb *bi* in the Jamaican Creole present tense:

Person	Subject	Verb Formation
First	mi	a
Second	yuh	a
Third	im, shi, ih/it*	a
Second (plural)	unnu	a
Third (plural)	dem, wi	a

*Note that *ih* is not used before *a*. E. *It* is used instead.

Here are some examples of Jamaican Creole sentences with their English meaning:

Jamaican Creole	English
Shi a̲ iih coz'n.	She is his cousin.
Tamieka a̲ mi bes fren.	Tamieka is my best friend.
Di uhman a̲ Canadian.	The woman is Canadian.

When the Verb Bi is Used Before Prepositions And Adverbs

The verb *bi* is irregular when used immediately before prepositions such as *a* (E. *at*), *pau* (E. *on*), *pan* (E. *on*), *inna* (E. *in*), *oova* (E, *over*), *anda* (E. *under*), etc., adverbs such as *ya* (E. *here*), *deh* (E. *there*), *dyer* (E. *there*), etc., that state the location or position of the subject. The verb becomes *deh* when used before them. In most cases, the sentence is usually stating the physical location or position of the subject.

Person	Subject	Verb Formation
First	mi	deh
Second	yuh	deh
Third	im, shi, ih/it	deh
Second (plural)	unnu	deh
Third (plural)	dem, wi	deh

Here are some examples of Jamaican Creole sentences with their English meaning:

Jamaican Creole	English
Sam <u>deh a</u> di paati.	Sam <u>is at</u> the party.
Im <u>deh inna</u> di store.	He <u>is in</u> the store.
Dem <u>deh anda</u> di umbrella.	They <u>are under</u> the umbrella.
Di skirt <u>deh pau</u> syel.	The skirt <u>is on</u> sale.

> A **preposition** is a word that shows the connection between a noun or pronoun and some other word or clause. Examples of prepositions include *above, below, by, on,* and *between.* In the example *John is on the table,* we can see where John (the noun) is in relation to the table (another noun). He is on it. *On* is the preposition in the sentence.

> An **adverb** is a word that modifies a verb, adjective, or another adverb. It can give information about the manner in which an action is done. It can also indicate time, place, or extent. Examples include *rather, slowly,* and *there.*

In the present tense of Jamaican Creole, the verb *bi* is sometimes omitted before prepositions such as *inna* (E. *in*), *oova* (E. *over*), *anda* (E. *under*), *dong* (E. *down*), *agens* (E. *against*), *afta* (E. *after*), and *aaf* (E. *off*). Here are some examples of Jamaican Creole sentences with their English meaning. As you can see in the English sentences, the verb is not omitted before the preposition:

Jamaican Creole	English
Sheena <u>inna</u> di store.	Sheena <u>is in</u> the store.
Dem <u>oova</u> deh.	They <u>are over</u> there.
Suzie <u>dong</u> a di bottom a di drive wyeh.	Suzie <u>is down</u> at the bottom of the driveway.

When the Verb Bi is Used with Adjectives

In Jamaican Creole, the verb *bi* is irregular when used with adjectives. In cases where the verb would be placed before an adjective in English, the verb is omitted in Jamaican Creole. Here are some examples of Jamaican Creole sentences with their English meaning. Notice in the English sentences that the verb *be* is not omitted:

Jamaican Creole	English
Di byebi <u>sick</u>.	The baby <u>is sick</u>.
Damion <u>happy</u>.	Damion <u>is happy</u>.
Ryan <u>taiyad</u>.	Ryan <u>is tired</u>.

> An **adjective** is a word that describes a noun or pronoun. Common examples of adjectives include *happy*, *sad*, *tired*, and *pretty*.

In Jamaican Creole, if an adverb is placed between the verb *bi* and the adjective, the verb *bi* is also omitted. Here are some examples of Jamaican Creole sentences with their English meaning. Notice in the English sentences that the verb *be* is not omitted:

Jamaican Creole	English
Wi <u>really serious</u>.	We <u>are really serious</u>.
Di daag <u>raada silly</u>.	The dog <u>is rather silly</u>.
Di food <u>especially good</u>.	The food <u>is especially good</u>.

Adjectives can describe a person's nationality. An example is *Patsy is Jamaican. Jamaican* is the adjective in this example. When an adjective describes a person's nationality in Jamaican Creole, the verb is usually used as *a*. The verb can also be omitted if the speaker chooses to omit it. Here are some examples of Jamaican Creole sentences with their English meaning. Notice in the English sentences that the verb *be* is not omitted:

Jamaican Creole	English
Sanjay <u>a</u> Trinidadian.	Sanjay <u>is</u> Trinidadian.
Shi Barbadian.	She [<u>is</u>] Barbadian.
Mackie a Jamaican.	Mackie <u>is</u> Jamaican.

When the Verb Bi Occurs At the End of a Sentence

The verb *bi* is irregular when it occurs at the end of a Jamaican Creole sentence. Sentences are rarely used in this format. In this case, the verb is used in its base infinitive form *bi*. Here are some examples of Jamaican Creole sentences with their English meaning:

Jamaican Creole	English
Deeh mek di matta muo difficult dan ih <u>bi</u>.	They make the matter more difficult than it <u>is</u>.
Who nuo wa deeh <u>bi</u>.	Who knows what they <u>are</u>.
Dat a weh dem <u>bi</u>.	That is what they <u>are</u>.

When Ih is Used with the Verb Bi Or Words Beginning Or Ending with the Letter A

The Jamaican Creole word *ih* is used to mean *it* in English. Jamaicans choose to use the English word *it* instead of the Jamaican Creole word *ih* in the following cases:

1. When *ih* occurs before and after the verb *a*.

2. When *ih* occurs before words beginning with the letter *a*.

3.   When *ih* occurs after words ending with the letter *a*.

Although Jamaicans sometimes use E. *it* in place of *ih*, both words are sometimes omitted when used at the beginning of a sentence before the verb *a*. Jamaicans typically say *It a di syem* or *A di syem* (E. *It is the same*).

Here are some examples of Jamaican Creole sentences with their English meaning:

Jamaican Creole	English
It a di bes.	It is the best.
A fidem.	It is theirs.
Dat a it.	That is it.

Practice Exercise 13

Translate the following sentences to Jamaican Creole, and determine whether to use *a*, *deh*, or *bi*.

1.   I am at work today.

_____

2.   Garfield and his friend are on the bus.

_____

3.   Jerry is the manager of the company.

_____

4.   The passengers are on the plane.

_____

5.   The book is on the shelf.

_____

6.   Their houses are far apart.

_____

7. That is what he wants.

   _____

8. The principal is in his office on the second floor of the building.

   _____

9. The paintings are on the wall.

   _____

10. The flowers are in a vase on the table.

   _____

Practice Exercise 14

Determine whether the following sentences make sense as they stand. Correct the ones that are incorrect by writing the correct sentence on the line.

1. Aalduo ᴱPeter deh a ᴱschool tudeh, im ᴱstill ᴱsick.

   _____

2. Dem a ᴱhappy.

   _____

3. Di ᴱemployee ᴱlike di manija, an iih ᴱhappy wid im ᴱjob.

   _____

4. Di pikini a ᴱhappy bikaah shi ᴱsmile wid aar madda.

   _____

5. ᴶDi sheet tear.

   _____

6. ᴱMiss ᴱPercy a di bes tiicha inna di ᴱschool.

   _____

7. ᴶDi student sad ᴶbikaah ᴶim get sixty percent ᴶpan ᴶim final exam.

   _____

26

8. Wi a di ong'l ᴱone dem weh deh ya.

_____

9. ᴱOutside daak.

_____

10. Pedro ʲa Guatemalan.

_____

Practice Exercise 15

Translate all sentences from Practice Exercise 14 to English. Make sure all sentences are grammatically correct.

1. _____
2. _____
3. _____
4. _____
5. _____
6. _____
7. _____
8. _____
9. _____
10. _____

Practice Exercise 16

Identify the Jamaican Creole word or words in the following sentences. Write the word or words on the line.

1. We are good pan Mathematics an English. _____

2. The child does not know what ih is. _____

3. Trina and Gerald a cousins. _____

4. Paula a the person weh in charge of the building.
   _____

5. I am happy fi be home today. _____

6. Jessica and Terry deh ya very often. _____

7. The books are on top of di piano. _____

8. The money is inna the handbag. _____

9. The hummingbird deh pan the winda. _____

10. The door opin. _____

Practice Exercise 17

Write the English words for the Jamaican Creole words you identified in Practice Exercise 16. Write the English word or words on the line.

1. We are good pan Mathematics an English. _____

2. The child does not know what ih is. _____

3. Trina and Gerald a cousins. _____

4. Paula a the person weh in charge of the building.
   _____

5. I am happy fi be home today. _____

6. Jessica and Terry deh ya very often. _____

7. The books are on top of di piano. _____

8. The money is inna the handbag. _____

9. The hummingbird deh pan the winda. _____

10. The door opin. _____

Practice Exercise 18

Use the verb *bi* along with the following words to form sentences in the simple present tense of Jamaican Creole. Identify the part of speech of the word you used by writing it on the line (e.g. noun, verb, etc.).

a soh *v. phrase* that is how; that is what   **juk** *n., v.* prick
badmain *adj., n.* envy; envious   **kyaar** *n.* car
chuo *n., v.* throw   **mowli** *adj.* moldy
gi *v.* give   **noweh** *adv., n.* nowhere

1. _____

   Part of speech _____

2. _____

   Part of speech _____

3. _____

   Part of speech _____

4. _____

   Part of speech _____

5. _____

   Part of speech _____

6. _____

   Part of speech _____

7. _____

   Part of speech _____

8. _____

   Part of speech _____

The Present Continuous Tense

The Present Continuous Tense of English

The present continuous tense tells us what is taking place at the current moment. The present continuous tense of English is formed by using the present form of the verb *be* with the main verb ending in –ing. The following table shows the formation of some verbs in the English present continuous tense:

Person	Subject	Verb Formation
First	I	am running
Second	you	are playing
Third	he, she, it	is studying
Second (plural)	you	are reading
Third (plural)	they, we	are doing

The Present Continuous Tense of Jamaican Creole

In Jamaican Creole, the present continuous tense is formed using the present tense of the verb *bi* (which is *a*) and the base infinitive form of the main verb. The following table shows the formation of verbs in the Jamaican Creole present continuous tense:

Person	Subject	Verb Formation	English Meaning
First	mi	a run	am running
Second	yuh	a plyeh	are playing
Third	im, shi, ih/it	a study	is studying
Second (plural)	unnu	a read	are reading
Third (plural)	dem, wi	a duh	are doing

Here are some examples of Jamaican Creole sentences with their English meaning:

Jamaican Creole	English
Sharon a goh a St. Mary.	Sharon is going to St. Mary.
Suzette a chuo out di gyabij.	Suzette is throwing out the garbage.
Dem a laugh.	They are laughing.
Di girl a cry.	The girl is crying.

In parts of Jamaica, the present tense of the verb *bi* is formed as *deh* when used in the present continuous tense. So, for the above examples, one would say:

Jamaican Creole	English
Sharon deh goh a St. Mary.	Sharon is going to St. Mary.
Suzette deh chuo out di gyabij.	Suzette is throwing out the garbage.
Dem deh laugh.	They are laughing.
Di girl deh cry.	The girl is crying.

Describing Multiple Actions

In English, if more than one action or event are occurring at the same time, it is not necessary to repeat the verb *be* with each verb. An example of this is *The children are hopping and skipping.* As you can see, *are* is only used before *hopping.* The same formation is used in Jamaican Creole, but the verb *bi* can also be repeated with the second verb. Here are some examples of Jamaican Creole sentences with their English meaning:

Jamaican Creole	English
Di family <u>a iht an drink</u>.	The family <u>is eating and drinking</u>.
Di student <u>a listen an andastan</u>.	The student <u>is listening and understanding</u>.
Di pikni dem <u>a run an a jump</u>.	The children <u>are running and [are] jumping</u>.

A form of the English present continuous tense is sometimes used in Jamaican Creole. In this formation of the present continuous tense, the verb *bi* is omitted, and only the present participle of the main verb ending in *-ing* is used. Here are some examples of Jamaican Creole sentences with their English meaning:

Jamaican Creole	English
Dem <u>spending</u> time ya.	They <u>are spending</u> time here.
Jim <u>going</u> to Clarendon.	Jim <u>is going</u> to Clarendon.
Im <u>laughing</u>.	He <u>is laughing</u>.

Irregular Verbs Sidong And Tan-op

In English, the Jamaican verbs *sidong* and *tan-op* mean *sit* and *stand*, respectively. The following table shows the formation of the verbs *sit* and *stand* in the English present continuous tense:

Person	Subject	English Verb Formation of Sit	English Verb Formation of Stand
First	I	am sitting	am standing
Second	you	are sitting	are standing
Third	he, she, it	is sitting	is standing
Second (plural)	you	are sitting	are standing
Third (plural)	they, we	are sitting	are standing

32

In Jamaican Creole, the verbs *sidong* (E. *sit*) and *tan-op* (E. *stand*) are exceptions to the regular formation of verbs in the present continuous tense. These verbs are formed like the simple present tense. Therefore, if one wanted to say *They are sitting over there* or *They are standing over there,* one would say *Deeh sidong oova dehsoh* or *Deeh tan-op oova dehsoh.*

The following table shows the formation of the verbs *sidong* and *tan-op* in the Jamaican Creole present continuous tense:

Person	Subject	Jamaican Creole Verb Formation of Sidong	English Meaning	Jamaican Creole Verb Formation of Tan-op	English Meaning
First	mi	sidong	am sitting	tan-op	am standing
Second	yuh	sidong	are sitting	tan-op	are standing
Third	im, shi, ih/it	sidong	is sitting	tan-op	is standing
Second (plural)	unnu	sidong	are sitting	tan-op	are standing
Third (plural)	dem, wi	sidong	are sitting	tan-op	are standing

If one were to say *Im a tan-op oova dehsoh,* it would mean that the speaker is saying that the person will be standing in the position or place at some point in the future, or that the person should be in the stated position because that is where they belong. (*The future tense is discussed later.*)

Practice Exercise 19

Translate the following sentences to English.

1. Di work_ja dem a bil wau ^Ebridge oova di riva.

   _____

2. Di ^Estudent dem a ^Etravel goh a ^ECuba pau wau ^Estudent ^Eexchange ^Eprogram.

   _____

3. Wi taiyad, ^Ebut wi a tek di ^Estairs dem.

   _____

4. ^JDi family ^Ja head ^Ja ^Jdi beach ^Jinna Ocho Rios.

   _____

5. Anita ^Ja learn well, but ^Jshi need ^Jfi study ^Jmuo.

   _____

6. Di bod a ^Efly oova di ^Ehill.

   _____

7. Aalduo di ^Esky ^Eclear inna ^ESt. Thomas, ryen a ^Efall inna ^EKingston.

   _____

8. Dem a ^Ecome oova ^Esoon,^E but mi a ^Eleave fi ^ESt. Elizabeth.

   _____

9. Wi a ha ^Elunch a di ^Enew ^Eseafood ^Erestaurant.

   _____

10. ^EAnna-Kay a ^Ehelp aar madda fi ^Ecook dinna.

    _____

Practice Exercise 20

Translate the following sentences to English, and underline the verb or verbs in the present continuous tense.

1. ᴱKeisha a styeh a di ᴱhouse wid aar bredda an aar sista.

   _____

2. Mi an ᴱSherry a goh a di shuo ᴱtomorrow maanin.

   _____

3. ᴱShaniece a ᴱsleep pan di ᴱcouch inna di ᴱliving ᴱroom, an aar sista a ᴱsleep inna di ᴱbedroom.

   _____

4. Di pikini a ᴱbrush im ᴱteeth.

   _____

5. Missa ᴱJoe a ᴱweed di ᴱgrass an a ᴱplant flowaz.

   _____

6. Di ᴱbook dem a jap aaf a di ᴱshelf.

   _____

7. Wi a ᴱhang di pikcha pan di ᴱwall.

   _____

8. Di daag a ᴱrun afta di ᴱcat.

   _____

9. ᴱLeroy a ᴱstudy fi im tes ᴱtomorrow.

   _____

10. ᴱJerome an ᴱKerona a goh a di ᴱbeach wid dem ᴱfamily.

    _____

Practice Exercise 21

Identify the Jamaican Creole phrase in the following sentences. Write the phrase on the line.

1. He is leaving tudeh wid im madda and his father.
    _____

2. Darren a goh weh tomorrow and is taking his pet.
    _____

3. Di byebi is playing in the crib. _____

4. We are studying fi di tes. _____

5. The man is mowing the lawn and a cut dong the bushes.
    _____

6. The tree that is standing pan di side a di ruod is growing.
    _____

7. She is moving nex mont. _____

8. I ha wok fi duh inna the yard, but it is getting dark.
    _____

9. The dog is barking afta di shadow of the tree.
    _____

10. I am going to the beach wid mi family. _____

Practice Exercise 22

Write the English phrase for each Jamaican Creole phrase you identified in the previous lesson on the line.

1. He is leaving tudeh wid im madda and his father.
    _____

2. Darren a goh weh tomorrow and is taking his pet.
    _____

3. Di byebi is playing in the crib. _____

4. We are studying fi di tes. _____

5. The man is mowing the lawn and a cut dong the bushes.
   _____

6. The tree that is standing pan di side a di ruod is growing.
   _____

7. She is moving nex mont. _____

8. I ha wok fi duh inna the yard, but it is getting dark.
   _____

9. The dog is barking afta di shadow of the tree.
   _____

10. I am going to the beach wid mi family. _____

Practice Exercise 23

Fill in the blanks with the Jamaican Creole present continuous form
of the verbs in brackets. Some of the verbs are in Jamaican Creole and
some are in English.

1. ᴱLuke _____ ᴱto di dyehkyer cent‚a fi ᴱpick ᴱup im
   pikini. (drive)

2. Wi _____ di ᴱbus fi goh a ᴱschool dis maanin. (tek)

3. ᴱJody an aar fren _____ pan di ᴱchoir. (sing)

4. ᴶDem _____ ᴶwau big piece ᴶa plank wood. (carry)

5. ᴱTrina _____ di grong wid wau ᴱstick. (juk)

6. Nof ᴱpeople _____ a ᴱsports dyeh dis mont. (come)

7. Shi _____ pan di ᴱside a di ruod ᴱuntil di ᴱtruck
   ᴱpass. (tan-op)

8. Junior _____ fish ᴶfi dinner ᴶtudeh ᴶan tomorrow. (catch)

37

9. ᴱSheila an ᴱPetrina _____ di syem ᴱdress goh a di paati. (wear)

10. It _____ ʲdaak outside. (get)

Pratcice Exercise 24

Translate the sentences you completed in Practice Exercise 23 to English. Underline the verbs in the present continuous tense.

1. _____
2. _____
3. _____
4. _____
5. _____
6. _____
7. _____
8. _____
9. _____
10. _____

Practice Exercise 25

Use the following words to form sentences in the present continuous tense of Jamaican Creole. Identify the part of speech of the word you used by writing it on the line (e.g. noun, verb, etc.).

aal now *adv. phrase* even now
ben *n., v.* bend
dehsoh *adv., n.* there
fi *prep., mod. aux.* for; should; ought to; to

kip *v.* keep
nomo *adv.* no more; any longer
ol *adj.* old

1. _____

   Part of speech _____

2. _____

   Part of speech _____

3. _____

   Part of speech _____

4. _____

   Part of speech _____

5. _____

   Part of speech _____

6. _____

   Part of speech _____

7. _____

   Part of speech _____

The Simple Past Tense

The Simple Past Tense of English

The simple past tense of English describes an action that has already taken place. Some verbs are regular and some are irregular in the simple past tense. Regular English verbs end in –ed. Irregular verbs do not have a consistent formation.

Here are some examples of regular verbs in the English past tense:

attended	followed	opened
carved	handled	pulled
destroyed	listened	voted

Here are some examples of irregular verbs in the English past tense:

bore	fought	knew
crept	gave	rode
drew	hid	tore

The Simple Past Tense of Jamaican Creole

The simple past tense of Jamaican Creole is formed differently than the simple past tense of English. There are primarily five ways to state something so that it is understood that the action or event occurred in the past. In a previous lesson, you learned that the simple present tense of Jamaican Creole is formed by using the same form of the verb for all subjects of the verb, whether singular or plural. This same principle applies to the simple past tense, except how far in the past the action occurred also determines how it is stated. Actions that occurred in the distant past are thought of differently than actions that occurred in the recent past (close to the present moment).

It can be formed in the following ways:

1. *Did* (also used as *beeh, weeh, beeh did*, or *weeh did*) is placed before the base infinitive form of the verb to indicate that the action occurred and was completed in the past. People in different parishes of the island might use one or more of these words. Let us imagine that someone had some food hours ago and is no longer eating. This action was already completed in the past. We would therefore use the past tense outlined below.

When the Past Tense is Formed with Did

Person	Subject	JC. verb iht	E. eat
First	mi	did iht	ate
Second	yuh	did iht	ate
Third	im, shi, ih/it	did iht	ate
Second (plural)	unnu	did iht	ate
Third (plural)	dem, wi	did iht	ate

When the Past Tense is Formed with Beeh

Person	Subject	JC. Verb iht	E. eat
First	mi	beeh iht	ate
Second	yuh	beeh iht	ate

Person	Subject	JC. Verb iht	E. eat
Third	im, shi, ih/it	beeh iht	ate
Second (plural)	unnu	beeh iht	ate
Third (plural)	dem, wi	beeh iht	ate

When the Past Tense is Formed with Weeh

Person	Subject	JC. verb iht	E. eat
First	mi	weeh iht	ate
Second	yuh	weeh iht	ate
Third	im, shi, ih/it	weeh iht	ate
Second (plural)	unnu	weeh iht	ate
Third (plural)	dem, wi	weeh iht	ate

When the Past Tense is Formed with Beeh Did

Person	Subject	JC. verb iht	E. eat
First	mi	beeh did iht	ate
Second	yuh	beeh did iht	ate
Third	im, shi, ih/it	beeh did iht	ate
Second (plural)	unnu	beeh did iht	ate
Third (plural)	dem, wi	beeh did iht	ate

When the Past Tense is Formed with Weeh Did

Person	Subject	JC. verb iht	E. eat
First	mi	weeh did iht	ate
Second	yuh	weeh did iht	ate

Person	Subject	JC. verb iht	E. eat
Third	im, shi, ih/it	weeh did iht	ate
Second (plural)	unnu	weeh did iht	ate
Third (plural)	dem, wi	weeh did iht	ate

Here are some examples of Jamaican Creole sentences with their English meaning:

Jamaican Creole	English
Ian <u>did goh</u> a wok.	Ian <u>went</u> to work.
Wi <u>beeh did tink</u> im sad.	We <u>thought</u> he was sad.
Di two tiicha dem <u>weeh meet</u> inna di staffroom.	The two teachers <u>met</u> in the staffroom.

In English, when a sentence contains two or more clauses (whether two independent clauses or a dependent clause and an independent clause), verbs of all clauses are used in the past tense if all actions took place in the past. An example is *Yesterday, my brother and I <u>went</u> to the park, and my brother <u>saw</u> his friends there.* As you can see, both verbs (*go* and *see*) are used in the past tense.

In Jamaican Creole, when a sentence has two clauses (whether it is two independent clauses or an independent clause and a dependent clause), one verb is often used in the past tense to make the rest of the sentence past. The present form of the other verb or verbs are used, even if it is being communicated that other action or actions also took place in the past. If the sentence has a dependent and an independent clause, the verb used in the independent clause is the one that is usually formed in the past tense.

A **clause** is a phrase with a subject and a predicate. An independent clause can stand on its own, but a dependent clause needs an independent clause to make sense. An example of an independent clause is *He has to leave now.* An example of a dependent clause is *Although he wants to stay.* If we put them together, the dependent clause would make sense: *He has to leave now, although he wants to stay.*

Here are some examples of Jamaican Creole sentences with their English meaning:

Jamaican Creole	English
Jason <u>did feel</u> taiyad afta im workout, soh im <u>goh</u> lie dong.	Jason <u>felt</u> tired after his workout, so he <u>went</u> to lie down.
Mi <u>weeh did goh</u> a St. Mary, auh mi sista <u>goh</u> a Spanish Town.	I <u>went</u> to St. Mary, and my sister <u>went</u> to Spanish Town.
Daryl auh Andre <u>beeh mek</u> wau deal, soh dem <u>shyek</u> han.	Daryl and Andre <u>made</u> a deal, so they <u>shook</u> hands.

Jamaicans sometimes use verbs in the dependent and the independent clause in the past tense, however. For example:

Sheila <u>did goh</u> a di paati, aalduo aar hosban <u>did goh</u> a wok (E. Sheila <u>went</u> to the party, although her husband <u>went</u> to work), or *Sheila <u>did goh</u> a di paati, aalduo aar hosban goh a wok* (E. Sheila <u>went</u> to the party, although her husband <u>went</u> to work). Both sentences are typically used in Jamaican Creole.

2. In Jamaican Creole, if the time that the action or event took place is mentioned, the need to put *did, beeh, weeh, beeh did*, or *weeh did* before the verb to form its past tense is optional. By letting the listener know when the action or event took place, the speaker can use the present tense, and the listener will understand that the action or event took place in the past.

Here are some examples of Jamaican Creole sentences with their English meaning:

Jamaican Creole	English
Laas Tuesday, wi <u>iht</u> a di restaurant.	lit. Last Tuesday, we <u>eat</u> at the restaurant. *(Last Tuesday, we ate at the restaurant.)*
Yessideh, mi family <u>goh</u> a riva.	lit. Yesterday, my family <u>go</u> to the river. *(Yesterday, my family went to the river.)*
Wedyeh, mi <u>goh</u> a mi anti house.	lit. The other day, I <u>go</u> to my aunt's house. *(The other day, I went to my aunt's house.)*

44

Note that Jamaicans sometimes use *did, beeh, weeh, beeh did*, or *weeh did* to form the past tense of a verb even if the time that the action or event took place in the past is mentioned. An example is *Yessideh, wi did goh a di zoo* (E. *Yesterday, we went to the zoo*).

3. When it has already been stated that the actions or events being discussed took place at a time in the past, the present tense is often used to tell the rest of the story or idea. For example, if you ask someone what they did yesterday and they were in school, they might respond:

Jamaican Creole

Mi did deh a school. Di tiicha teach wau new topic. Shi talk bout di Taino dem auh di wyeh dem faam. Shi seh wi fi research di topic muo auh come back wid wau shaat essay.

English

Literal Meaning

I was at school. The teacher teaches a new topic. She talks about the Tainos and the way they farm. She says we should research the topic more and come back with a short essay.

Actual Meaning

I was at school. The teacher taught a new topic. She talked about the Tainos and the way they farmed. She said we should research the topic more and come back with a short essay.

In the English example, all verbs that describe actions that took place in the past (*be, teach, talk, form, say,* and *play*) are used in the past tense.

4. When an action began in the past, but some aspect of the action is still occurring up to the present moment, the simple present tense is frequently used.

Here are some examples of Jamaican Creole sentences with their English meaning:

Jamaican Creole	English
Di Police Force <u>styeshan</u> the policeman a Montego Bay.	lit. The Police Force <u>stations</u> the policeman in Montego Bay. (*The Police Force stationed the policeman in Montego Bay.*)
Mi faada <u>fix</u> di pipe, but it a leak.	lit. My father <u>fixes</u> the pipe, but it is leaking. (*My father fixed the pipe, but it is leaking.*)
Suzie <u>iht</u> di food an <u>lef</u> di plyet inna di kitchen sink.	lit. Suzie <u>eats</u> the food and <u>leaves</u> the plate in the kitchen sink. (*Suzie ate the food and left the plate in the kitchen sink.*)

As you can see in the examples, all verbs used in English to describe actions that took place in the past are formed in the past tense. The Jamaican Creole verbs are formed in the present tense because some aspect of the event is occurring in the present moment. For example, in the first sentence, we can assume that the policeman is still stationed in Montego Bay up to the present moment.

5. If an action or event recently happened and ended right before the present moment, such as immediately before the speaker spoke about it, the simple present tense is frequently used in Jamaican Creole to talk about the event or action. In English, even if the action or event occurred less than a second ago, once it occurred and was completed, the past tense is used. Here are some examples of Jamaican Creole sentences with their English meaning. Imagine that these events happened just a second ago:

Jamaican Creole	English
Shakira <u>chuo-weh</u> di milk pan di floor.	lit. Shakira <u>spills</u> the milk on the floor. (*Shakira spilled the milk on the floor.*)

Jamaican Creole	English
Byron <u>look</u> pau yuh.	lit. Byron <u>looks</u> at you.
	(*Byron looked at you.*)
Jevon <u>tek</u> ih out a iih pakit.	lit. Jevon <u>takes</u> it out of his pocket.
	(*Jevon took it out of his pocket.*)

Practice Exercise 26

Translate the following sentences to English. Sentences should be in the past tense.

1. Sooh ^Estudent ^Ecome afta di ^Eclass staat.

   _____

2. Dennis get to ^Jdi ^Jshuo ^Jpan time.

   _____

3. ^EWhen mi ^Elook ^Eup pan di ^Esky, ih ^Elook daak.

   _____

4. Im ^Etalk wid im madda bout di ^Ehistory a di ^Ecountry.

   _____

5. ^JDi house look white when ^Jdem did ^Jpyent ^Jih, but now ^Jih look yellow.

   _____

6. ^JWau tree fall ^Jyessideh, ^Jan ^Jwaunedda one fall again ^Jtudeh.

   _____

7. Di ^Ebus ^Ecarry passinja goh a ^Etown.

   _____

8. ^ETen dyeh agoh, ^ERanjay dash-weh ^Ecoffee pan im ^Eshirt, auh di styen ^Estill deh deh.

   _____

9. When ᴶmi visit ᴶmi ᴶsista ᴶinna Peru, ᴶwi visit ᴶdi capital city Lima.

   _____

10. Di daag chyes afta wau stryeh ᴱcat.

   _____

Practice Exercise 27

The following sentences should be in the simple past tense. Rewrite each sentence in the forms of the simple past tense you learned about. Try to imagine that the action or event took place at some time in the past (recent or farther in the past), and you are telling this to another person.

1. Mi iht inna di iivlin, soh mi ᴱfull.

   _____

   _____

   _____

   _____

   _____

2. Wi did ᴱlie dong pan di ᴱbeach ᴱwhile ryen a ᴱfall, an wi ᴱget ᴱwet.

   _____

   _____

   _____

   _____

3. Shi lef yessideh.

   _____

   _____

_____

_____

_____

4. Di winda beeh did opin, an di ryen ^Ewet di ^Ebed.

_____

_____

_____

_____

5. Dem plyeh pan di ^Eteam ^Ewhen mi faada goh a ^Ehigh ^Eschool.

_____

_____

_____

_____

6. Jos ^Enow, iih pyent di ^Ewall.

_____

_____

_____

_____

7. Mi tink iih did ^Eserious ^Ewhen iih did seh soh.

_____

_____

_____

_____

8. Di byebi did ^Ecry ^Ewhen iih madda did lef.

_____

_____

_____

_____

_____

9. Shi weeh blyem im fi fyel aar ^Eexam dem.

_____

_____

_____

_____

10. Aar madda gi aar ^Efifty dalla bifuo shi goh a ^Eschool
    dis maanin.

_____

_____

_____

_____

_____

Practice Exercise 28

Use the following list of verb phrases to form Jamaican Creole sentences of your own. Use each verb phrase only once.

| did si | beeh ^Etell | weeh ^Ehelp | beeh did ^Ecarry | weeh did opin |
| did ^Efeel | beeh uo | weeh ^Eread | beeh did ^Epull | weeh did shuo |

1. _____

2. _____

3. _____

4. _____

5. _____

6. _____

7. _____

8. _____

9. _____

10. _____

Practice Exercise 29

Translate the Jamaican Creole sentences from Practice Exercise 28 to English.

1. _____

2. _____

3. _____

4. _____

5. _____

6. _____

7. _____

8. _____

9. _____

10. _____

Practice Exercise 30

Circle the verb in the simple past tense for each sentence, and then rewrite the sentence in English.

1. ᴱNicholas beeh ᴱtravel wid im ᴱwife an pikini dem goh a ᴱCanada fi ᴱvacation.

   _____

2. Di ᴱpolice dem weeh ᴱsurround di ᴱbuilding an ᴱtell ᴱeverybody fi ᴱexit.

   _____

3. ᴱLashawna did a di fos uhman fi ᴱwin wau ᴱtrophy inna di ᴱcompetition.

   _____

4. ᴱTen a di ᴱred ᴱbubble-gum dem an ᴱtwo a di ᴱblue ᴱone dem beeh did jap pan di grong.

   _____

5. Mi madda seh di gryep dem noh ᴱgood, ᴱbut yessideh dem did ᴱripe an ᴱjuicy.

   _____

6. ᴱTwo dyeh agoh, wi goh a di riva.

   _____

7. Dem weeh did aks mi fi goh wid dem a di ᴱstore.

   _____

8. ᴱJacky beeh ᴱtell wi fi ᴱstudy fi di ᴱexam ᴱone ᴱmonth agoh.

   _____

9. ᴱAaron beeh did si di myelᴱman weh diliva myel ᴱalong wi ᴱstreet.

   _____

10. Di ᴱtree weeh ᴱneed waata fi gruo.

   _____

Practice Exercise 31

Use the following words to form sentences in the simple past tense of Jamaican Creole. Identify the part of speech of the word you used by writing it on the line (e.g. noun, verb, etc.).

adda *adj., adv., pron.* other
baada *n., v.* border
hyeh *v.* hear
laba *v.* to talk excessively

si *v.* see
taiyadin *adj.* tiring
uolbrok *n.* secondhand clothes;
anything used

1. _____

   Part of speech _____

2. _____

   Part of speech _____

3. _____

   Part of speech _____

4. _____

   Part of speech _____

5. _____

   Part of speech _____

6. _____

   Part of speech _____

7. _____

   Part of speech _____

The Verb Bi in the Simple Past Tense

The past formation of the English verb *be* is outlined in the table below. The verb is irregular in the English past tense.

Person	Subject	Verb Formation
First	I	was
Second	you	were
Third	he, she, it	was
Second (plural)	you	were
Third (plural)	they, we	were

The verb *bi* (E. *be*) is irregular in the simple past tense of Jamaican Creole. Its formation is *did a*. The verb is also formed *ben a*, *wen a*, *beeh did a*, or *weeh did a*, but these formations are less commonly used.

When Bi is Formed Did A

Person	Subject	Verb Formation	English Meaning
First	mi	did a	was
Second	yuh	did a	were
Third	im, shi, ih/it	did a	was
Second (plural)	unnu	did a	were
Third (plural)	dem, wi	did a	were

54

When Bi is Formed Ben A

Person	Subject	Verb Formation	English Meaning
First	mi	ben a	was
Second	yuh	ben a	were
Third	im, shi, ih/it	ben a	was
Second (plural)	unnu	ben a	were
Third (plural)	dem, wi	ben a	were

When Bi is Formed Wen A

Person	Subject	Verb Formation	English Meaning
First	mi	wen a	was
Second	yuh	wen a	were
Third	im, shi, ih/it	wen a	was
Second (plural)	unnu	wen a	were
Third (plural)	dem, wi	wen a	were

When Bi is Formed Beeh Did A

Person	Subject	Verb Formation	English Meaning
First	mi	beeh did a	was
Second	yuh	beeh did a	were
Third	im, shi, ih/it	beeh did a	was
Second (plural)	unnu	beeh did a	were
Third (plural)	dem, wi	beeh did a	were

When Bi is Formed Weeh Did A

Person	Subject	Verb Formation	English Meaning
First	mi	weeh did a	was
Second	yuh	weeh did a	were

Person	Subject	Verb Formation	English Meaning
Third	im, shi, ih/it	weeh did a	was
Second (plural)	unnu	weeh did a	were
Third (plural)	dem, wi	weeh did a	were

Here are some examples of Jamaican Creole sentences with their English meaning:

Jamaican Creole	English
Lea <u>did a</u> mi fren.	Lea <u>was</u> my friend.
Im <u>beeh did a</u> di bes kuoch mi ha.	He <u>was</u> the best coach I had.
Di man <u>wen a</u> St. Lucian.	The man <u>was</u> St. Lucian.

Reversing Did A

When using *did a* (but not *ben a*, *wen a*, *beeh did a*, or *weeh did a*), the format of the verb can be reversed. So, we can use *a did* where we would use *did a*. For example:

Jamaican Creole	English
David <u>a did</u> iih assistant.	David <u>was</u> his assistant.
Im <u>a did</u> di bes kuoch mi ha.	He <u>was</u> the best coach I had.
Di man <u>a did</u> St. Lucian.	The man <u>was</u> St. Lucian.

When the Verb Bi is Used Before Prepositions

The verb *bi* is also irregular when used directly before prepositions such as *a* (E. *at*), *pan* (E. *on*), *pau* (E. *on*), *inna* (E. *in*), *oova* (E, *over*), *anda* (E. *under*), *dong* (E. *down*), etc., and adverbs such as *ya* (E. *here*), *deh* (E. *there*), *dyer* (E. *there*), etc., that indicate position or location. The verb becomes *did deh* (also used as *beeh deh*, *weeh deh*, *beeh did deh*, or *weeh did deh*) when used before them. In most instances, the sentence is usually stating the physical location or position of the subject.

When Bi is Formed Did Deh

Person	Subject	Verb Formation	English Meaning
First	mi	did deh	was
Second	yuh	did deh	were
Third	im, shi, ih/it	did deh	was
Second (plural)	unnu	did deh	were
Third (plural)	dem, wi	did deh	were

When Bi is Formed Beeh Deh

Person	Subject	Verb Formation	English Meaning
First	mi	beeh deh	was
Second	yuh	beeh deh	were
Third	im, shi, ih/it	beeh deh	was
Second (plural)	unnu	beeh deh	were
Third (plural)	dem, wi	beeh deh	were

When Bi is Formed Weeh Deh

Person	Subject	Verb Formation	English Meaning
First	mi	weeh deh	was
Second	yuh	weeh deh	were
Third	im, shi, ih/it	weeh deh	was
Second (plural)	unnu	weeh deh	were
Third (plural)	dem, wi	weeh deh	were

When Bi is Formed Beeh Did Deh

Person	Subject	Verb Formation	English Meaning
First	mi	beeh did deh	was
Second	yuh	beeh did deh	were

Person	Subject	Verb Formation	English Meaning
Third	im, shi, ih/it	beeh did deh	was
Second (plural)	unnu	beeh did deh	were
Third (plural)	dem, wi	beeh did deh	were

When Bi is Formed Weeh Did Deh

Person	Subject	Verb Formation	English Meaning
First	mi	weeh did deh	was
Second	yuh	weeh did deh	were
Third	im, shi, ih/it	weeh did deh	was
Second (plural)	unnu	weeh did deh	were
Third (plural)	dem, wi	weeh did deh	were

Here are some examples of Jamaican Creole sentences with their English meaning:

Jamaican Creole	English
Di skirt <u>did deh pau</u> syel.	The skirt <u>was on</u> sale.
Jim <u>beeh did deh dong</u> by di seaside.	Jim <u>was down</u> by the seaside.
Di bag <u>did deh oova</u> dyer.	The bag <u>was over</u> there.
Di milk <u>weeh deh inna</u> di fridge.	The milk <u>was in</u> the fridge.

Despite this general rule, however, it is not uncommon for speakers of Jamaican Creole to shorten the verb, omitting *deh* before prepositions such as *inna* (E. *in*), *oova* (E. *over*), *anda* (E. *under*), *dong* (E. *down*), *agens* (E. *against*), *afta* (E. *after*), and *aaf* (E. *off*). *Did, beeh, weeh, beeh did,* and *weeh did* are not omitted before these prepositions. For example:

Jamaican Creole	English
Winston <u>did inna</u> di house.	Winston <u>was in</u> the house.
Di girl <u>beeh did oova</u> dyer.	The girl <u>was over</u> there.

Jamaican Creole	English
Di pen dem <u>did dong</u> a di bottom a di bag.	The pens <u>were down</u> at the bottom of the bag.
Wi <u>weeh aaf</u> a di bus when ih lik wau puol.	We <u>were off</u> the bus when it hit a pole.

Note that *deh* is not omitted in Jamaican Creole before these prepositions and adverbs: *a, pan, pau, deh, dyer,* and *ya.* For example:

Jamaican Creole	English
Trevor <u>did deh a</u> school when im bredda lef.	Trevor <u>was at</u> school when his brother left.
Di book <u>beeh deh pan</u> di shelf.	The book <u>was on</u> the shelf.
Di pikini <u>weeh did deh ya</u>.	The child <u>was here</u>.

When the Verb Bi is Used with Adjectives

The formation of the English verb *be* before adjectives is the same as its formation in sentences without adjectives. An example of its use is *She was happy.* In Jamaican Creole, the verb *bi* is irregular when used before adjectives and is shortened *did* (also used as *beeh, weeh, beeh did,* or *weeh did*) before them.

When Bi is Formed Did

Person	Subject	Verb Formation	English Meaning
First	mi	did	was
Second	yuh	did	were
Third	im, shi, ih/it	did	was
Second (plural)	unnu	did	were
Third (plural)	dem, wi	did	were

When Bi is Formed Beeh

Person	Subject	Verb Formation	English Meaning
First	mi	beeh	was
Second	yuh	beeh	were
Third	im, shi, ih/it	beeh	was
Second (plural)	unnu	beeh	were
Third (plural)	dem, wi	beeh	were

When Bi is Formed Weeh

Person	Subject	Verb Formation	English Meaning
First	mi	weeh	was
Second	yuh	weeh	were
Third	im, shi, ih/it	weeh	was
Second (plural)	unnu	weeh	were
Third (plural)	dem, wi	weeh	were

When Bi is Formed Beeh Did

Person	Subject	Verb Formation	English Meaning
First	mi	beeh did	was
Second	yuh	beeh did	were
Third	im, shi, ih/it	beeh did	was
Second (plural)	unnu	beeh did	were
Third (plural)	dem, wi	beeh did	were

When Bi is Formed Weeh Did

Person	Subject	Verb Formation	English Meaning
First	mi	weeh did	was
Second	yuh	weeh did	were

Person	Subject	Verb Formation	English Meaning
Third	im, shi, ih/it	weeh did	was
Second (plural)	unnu	weeh did	were
Third (plural)	dem, wi	weeh did	were

Here are some examples of Jamaican Creole sentences with their English meaning:

Jamaican Creole	English
Pam <u>did sick</u>.	Pam <u>was sick</u>.
Maurice did lose im house inna di faiya, an im <u>beeh did sad</u>.	Maurice lost his house in the fire, and he <u>was sad</u>.
Iih <u>weeh lonely</u>, soh iih get wau pet.	He <u>was lonely</u>, so he got a pet.

Note also, that if an adverb is placed between the verb *bi* and the adjective, the rule is still used. For example:

Jamaican Creole	English
Mi <u>did **buon** taiyad</u>.	I <u>was **bone** tired</u>.
Shi <u>beeh did **raada** happy</u>.	She <u>was **rather** happy</u>.
Dem <u>weeh **really** excited</u>.	They <u>were **really** excited.</u>

The verb is irregular when it occurs at the end of a sentence. Sentences are rarely used in this format, however. In this case, the verb is formed *did bi* (also used as *beeh bi, weeh bi, beeh did bi,* or *weeh did bi*).

When Bi is Formed Did Bi

Person	Subject	Verb Formation	English Meaning
First	mi	did bi	was
Second	yuh	did bi	were
Third	im, shi, ih/it	did bi	was
Second (plural)	unnu	did bi	were
Third (plural)	dem, wi	did bi	were

When Bi is Formed Beeh Bi

Person	Subject	Verb Formation	English Meaning
First	mi	beeh bi	was
Second	yuh	beeh bi	were
Third	im, shi, ih/it	beeh bi	was
Second (plural)	unnu	beeh bi	were
Third (plural)	dem, wi	beeh bi	were

When Bi is Formed Weeh Bi

Person	Subject	Verb Formation	English Meaning
First	mi	weeh bi	was
Second	yuh	weeh bi	were
Third	im, shi, ih/it	weeh bi	was
Second (plural)	unnu	weeh bi	were
Third (plural)	dem, wi	weeh bi	were

When Bi is Formed Beeh Did Bi

Person	Subject	Verb Formation	English Meaning
First	mi	beeh did bi	was
Second	yuh	beeh did bi	were
Third	im, shi, ih/it	beeh did bi	was
Second (plural)	unnu	beeh did bi	were
Third (plural)	dem, wi	beeh did bi	were

When Bi is Formed Weeh Did Bi

Person	Subject	Verb Formation	English Meaning
First	mi	weeh did bi	was
Second	yuh	weeh did bi	were

Person	Subject	Verb Formation	English Meaning
Third	im, shi, ih/it	weeh did bi	was
Second (plural)	unnu	weeh did bi	were
Third (plural)	dem, wi	weeh did bi	were

Here are some examples of Jamaican Creole sentences with their English meaning:

Jamaican Creole	English
Deeh did mek di matta muo difficult dan ih <u>did bi</u>.	They made the matter more difficult than it <u>was</u>.
Who nuo wa deeh <u>beeh did bi</u>.	Who knows what they <u>were</u>.
Dat a weh ih <u>weeh bi</u>.	That is what it <u>was</u>.

Practice Exercise 32

Translate the following sentences to English.

1. ^ETeresa an ^EShanakay did deh deh ^Eearly.

   _____

2. Di ruod did shaata ^Ea ^Eyear agoh.

   _____

3. Wi pyeh did ^Eless dan wi did tink ih shudda bi.

   _____

4. Di daansa dem did deh a di tyeta ^Eearly.

   _____

5. ^EShania did a di winna a di ^Eprize.

   _____

6. ^JDi new dress ^Jdem ^Jdid ^Jinna ^Jdi store when ^Jwi pass by.

   _____

7. Di bulla did inna di ᴱcupboard, ᴱbut ᴱnow ih ᴱgone.

_____

8. Di ᴱman did ᴱvery ᴱhappy ᴱwhen im granpikini ᴱcome fi siim.

_____

9. A did fidem ᴱjob fi ᴱclean di ᴱkitchen.

_____

10. Jessica ᴶdid very sad when ᴶaar ᴶdaag ᴶdid sick.

_____

Practice Exercise 33

Determine if the following sentences make sense as they stand. Correct the ones that are incorrect by writing the sentence on the line. The sentences should be in Jamaican Creole.

1. Di ᴱtreehouse beeh did pap dong ᴱfrom di ᴱtree.

_____

2. Shi did nuo weh ih a.

_____

3. ᴱKirk weeh ᴱsad seh iih fyel di tes.

_____

4. It ᴶa windy ᴶyessideh by ᴶdi sea.

_____

5. Di shuo ben a ᴱexciting.

_____

6. ᴱShawn an ᴱJimmy did a di ᴱtwo bes memba dem inna di ᴱclub.

_____

7. Port Antonio ᴶdid sunny.

_____

8. ^EGina did a mi bes fren inna ^Ehigh ^Eschool.

    _____

9. Di ^Eman dem beeh a a di paati.

    _____

10. ^EMisha did deh a di maakit.

    _____

Practice Exercise 34

Complete the following sentences by inserting the correct form of the verb *bi* on the line. Sentences should be in the simple past tense.

1. ^EDanny _____ a maakit yessideh.
2. ^JDi suitcase _____ heavy.
3. Shi _____ wid aar fren a di ^Eparade.
4. ^EJames _____ mi fren.
5. Wi _____ pan di wyeh a goh a ^EClarendon ^Ewhen ih ha'mn.
6. Di uhman _____ inna di ^Estore an di pikini _____ ^Eoutside.
7. Mrs. Patterson _____ ^Jdi ^Jtiicha ^Jfi class one.
8. ^EOne ^Eweek agoh, wi _____ a di ^Erestaurant.
9. Di pikini _____ ^Ehappy.
10. Ih _____ pan di tyeb'l ^Ewhen mi _____ huom.

Practice Exercise 35

Translate all sentences from Practice Exercise 34 to English.

1. _____
2. _____

3. _____

4. _____

5. _____

6. _____

7. _____

8. _____

9. _____

10. _____

Practice Exercise 36

Fill in the blanks with the most appropriate verb or verb phrase below.

beeh did deh   ben did a   weeh

1. Wi _____ ᴱout inna di yaad.

2. ᴱJulia seh shi _____ di ᴱheadgirl fi aar ᴱclass ᴱwhen shi _____ inna ᴱhigh ᴱschool.

3. Mi _____ ᴱglad seh mi madda did ᴱbuy mi wau ᴱnew ᴱpair a ᴱshoes.

4. Di pikcha _____ pan di ᴱwall.

5. Ih _____ oova inna ᴱten ᴱminutes.

6. Shi _____ ᴱtall ᴱwhen shi _____ wau likk'l ᴱgirl.

7. ᴶDi crowd _____ noisy.

8. Steven _____ one mile from ᴶim destination when ᴶim ᴶkyaar run out ᴶa fuel.

9. ᴱSam _____ ᴱdisappointed seh im neva ᴱreach im guol.

10. ᴶDi TV _____ ᴶpan ᴶdi sports channel.

Practice Exercise 37

Use the verb *bi* and the following words to form sentences in the simple past tense of Jamaican Creole. Use each word only once. Identify the part of speech of the word you used by writing it on the line (e.g. noun, verb, etc.).

aaf *adj. adv., n., prep.* off
blakkin *n.* hibiscus
chring *n., v.* string
duo-wyeh *n.* doorway

jinal *n.* trickster
niiv'n *adv. phrase* not even
ops *adj.* meddlesome

1. _____

   Part of speech _____

2. _____

   Part of speech _____

3. _____

   Part of speech _____

4. _____

   Part of speech _____

5. _____

   Part of speech _____

6. _____

   Part of speech _____

7. _____

   Part of speech _____

The Continuous Past Tense

The Continuous Past Tense of English

The continuous past tense tells us what was happening in the past. The action went on for a period of time in the past before coming to an end. In English, it is formed with the past tense of the verb *be* (*was* or *were*) and the main verb ending in –ing. Here are some examples of verbs in the continuous past tense:

Person	Subject	Verb Formation
First	I	was running
Second	you	were studying
Third	he, she, it	was playing
Second (plural)	you	were reading
Third (plural)	they, we	were doing

The Continous Past Tense of Jamaican Creole

In Jamaica Creole, the continuous past tense is formed by using the past tense of the verb *bi*, which is *did a* (also used as *ben a, wen a, did deh, beeh deh, weeh deh, beeh did deh,* or *weeh did deh*), with the base infinitive form of the main verb.

When the Continuous Past Tense is Formed with Did A

Person	Subject	Verb Formation	Englsih Meaning
First	mi	did a run	was running
Second	yuh	did a study	were studying
Third	im, shi, ih/it	did a plyeh	was playing
Second (plural)	unnu	did a read	were reading
Third (plural)	dem, wi	did a duh	were doing

When the Continuous Past Tense is Formed with Ben A

Person	Subject	Verb Formation	Englsih Meaning
First	mi	ben a run	was running
Second	yuh	ben a study	were studying
Third	im, shi, ih/it	ben a plyeh	was playing
Second (plural)	unnu	ben a read	were reading
Third (plural)	dem, wi	ben a duh	were doing

When the Continuous Past Tense is Formed with Wen A

Person	Subject	Verb Formation	Englsih Meaning
First	mi	wen a run	was running
Second	yuh	wen a study	were studying
Third	im, shi, ih/it	wen a plyeh	was playing
Second (plural)	unnu	wen a read	were reading
Third (plural)	dem, wi	wen a duh	were doing

When the Continuous Past Tense is Formed with Did Deh

Person	Subject	Verb Formation	Englsih Meaning
First	mi	did deh run	was running
Second	yuh	did deh study	were studying

Person	Subject	Verb Formation	Englsih Meaning
Third	im, shi, ih/it	did deh plyeh	was playing
Second (plural)	unnu	did deh read	were reading
Third (plural)	dem, wi	did deh duh	were doing

When the Continuous Past Tense is Formed with Beeh Deh

Person	Subject	Verb Formation	Englsih Meaning
First	mi	beeh deh run	was running
Second	yuh	beeh deh study	were studying
Third	im, shi, ih/it	beeh deh plyeh	was playing
Second (plural)	unnu	beeh deh read	were reading
Third (plural)	dem, wi	beeh deh duh	were doing

When the Continuous Past Tense is Formed with Weeh Deh

Person	Subject	Verb Formation	Englsih Meaning
First	mi	weeh deh run	was running
Second	yuh	weeh deh study	were studying
Third	im, shi, ih/it	weeh deh plyeh	was playing
Second (plural)	unnu	weeh deh read	were reading
Third (plural)	dem, wi	weeh deh duh	were doing

When the Continuous Past Tense is Formed with Beeh Did Deh

Person	Subject	Verb Formation	Englsih Meaning
First	mi	beeh did deh run	was running
Second	yuh	beeh did deh study	were studying
Third	im, shi, ih/it	beeh did deh plyeh	was playing
Second (plural)	unnu	beeh did deh read	were reading
Third (plural)	dem, wi	beeh did deh duh	were doing

When the Continuous Past Tense is Formed with Weeh Did Deh

Person	Subject	Verb Formation	Englsih Meaning
First	mi	weeh did deh run	was running
Second	yuh	weeh did deh study	were studying
Third	im, shi, ih/it	weeh did deh plyeh	was playing
Second (plural)	unnu	weeh did deh read	were reading
Third (plural)	dem, wi	weeh did deh duh	were doing

Here are some examples of Jamaican Creole sentences with their English meaning:

Jamaican Creole	English
Shiona did a run.	Shiona was running.
Im beeh did deh clean di room.	He was cleaning the room.
Maas Jim wen a pyent laas night.	Mr. Jim was painting last night.

Irregular Verbs Sidong And Tan-op

The verbs *sidong* (E. *sit*) and *tan-op* (E. *stand*) are exceptions to the regular formation of verbs in the continuous past tense of Jamaican Creole. These verbs are formed like the simple past tense that uses *did, beeh, weeh, beeh did,* and *weeh did.* For example:

Jamaican Creole	English
Jevon an Kiesha did sidong oova dehsoh.	Jevon and Kiesha were sitting over there.
Deeh beeh tan-op inna di crowd.	They were standing in the crowd.
Miss Jenny weeh did tan-op pan di varanda.	Miss Jenny was standing on the veranda.

Practice Exercise 38

Translate the following sentences to English.

1. Di ^{E}girl dem wen a ^{E}dance a di ^{E}talent shuo yessideh.

   _____

2. Shi did bihain inna aar wok, soh shi did a wok oova$_E$time.

   _____

3. Shi did a ^{E}clean aar ^{E}closet.

   _____

4. Wi weeh deh ^{E}leave di paak ^{E}when di kyaar ^{E}speed ^{E}by.

   _____

5. Wi beeh sidong inna di ^{E}dining ^{E}room bikaah di ^{E}living ^{E}room did ^{E}messy.

   _____

6. Dem did a tek wau ^{E}long ^{E}time.

   _____

7. ^{E}Gavin ben a ^{E}sleep inna wau ^{E}hammock a di ^{E}back a di ^{E}house.

   _____

8. Wi did a ^{E}help di ^{E}charity aaganaizyeshan fi ^{E}distribute ^{E}clothes ^{E}to di ^{E}needy.

   _____

9. Di pikini dem beeh deh plyeh inna di yaad.

   _____

10. Di riva did a fluo ^{E}heavy bikaah ryen did a ^{E}fall.

    _____

Practice Exercise 39

Translate the following sentences to English, and underline all verbs used in the continuous past tense.

1. Ih did a ^Eget lyet ^Ewhen wi did a ^Eleave ^Eschool.

   _____

2. Di pikini ben a ^Eget ^Eready fi goh a ^Eclass.

   _____

3. Di ^Emango dem did deh jap pan di ^Eroof a di ^Ehouse.

   _____

4. ^EShakira weeh did deh ^Eput aar ^Ebag inna di ^Ecloset inna aar ^Eroom.

   _____

5. Mi did a ^Eget ^Eready fi goh a ^Etown.

   _____

6. Di tiicha wen a pyes pyepa pan di ^Ewall.

   _____

7. Di pikni dem did a plyeh inna di yaad.

   _____

8. Di guot did deh iht ^Egrass ^Eout inna di grong.

   _____

9. Wi weeh deh ^Ewatch ^Etelevision ^Ewhen wau ^Fball brok chruu di winda.

   _____

10. Di ^Emeat tyes ^Efunny bikaah ih did a bon.

   _____

Practice Exercise 40

Fill in the blanks with the most appropriate verb from the list below. Use the verbs in the continuous past tense.

talk	fly	fix	run	watch	cut
sell	measure	mow	fall	grease	eat

1. Kenielia _____ on the field.

2. The man _____ corn in the tuck-shop.

3. They _____ the roof before it began to rain.

4. Jessica and Joe _____ in the hallway when the teacher saw them.

5. The students _____ a documentary in the audio-visual room.

6. The baker _____ the ingredients for the cake and _____ the baking tins.

7. The rain _____ steadily outside my window.

8. Pete _____ the lawn and _____ the branches.

9. Donna and Jenny _____ to Miami next week.

10. I _____ ice-cream on a hot summer day.

Practice Exercise 41

Underline the verbs in the continuous past tense in the following sentences.

1. Di bwuay did a ᴱfeed di ᴱpigeon dem weh deh pan di ᴱstreet.

2. Wi wen a ᴱpractice fi ᴱsing pan wi wyeh goh a ᴱschool.

3. ᴱJudy beeh deh sidong pan di ᴱsidewalk bikaah shi taiyad.

4. ᴱSuzie an ᴱErrol weeh deh ᴱclean di winda an di ᴱdoor dem.

5. Di pikini dem ben a ᴱwatch ᴱTV inna dem ᴱroom.

6. ᴱGranny did a waata di ᴱplant dem ᴱout inna di gyaad'n ᴱwhen di ryen staat ᴱfall.

7. Mi weeh deh expek fi ᴱpass ᴱall a mi ᴱexam dem.

8. Di ᴱteam did a win di gyem, ᴱbut den dem ᴱlose.

9. Ih did a ᴱget ᴱhot inna di ᴱhouse.

10. Di ᴱstudent dem did a ᴱget ᴱwet inna di ryen ᴱwhile dem did deh pan di fiil.

Practice Exercise 42

Translate all sentences from Practice Exercise 41 to English.

1. _____

2. _____

3. _____

4. _____

5. _____

6. _____

7. _____

8. _____

9. _____

10. _____

Practice Exercise 43

Use the following words to form sentences in the continuous past tense of Jamaican Creole. Identify the part of speech of the word you used by writing it on the line (e.g. noun, verb, etc.).

aada *n., v.* order
ajos *v.* adjust
bifuo *adv., conj., prep.* before
doppi *n.* ghost

eniweh *adv., pron.* anywhere
faak *n., v.* fork
gaaliin *n.* egret

1. _____

    Part of speech _____

2. _____

    Part of speech _____

3. _____

    Part of speech _____

4. _____

    Part of speech _____

5. _____

    Part of speech _____

6. _____

    Part of speech _____

7. _____

    Part of speech _____

The Present Perfect Tense

The Present Perfect Tense of English

The present perfect tense of English is formed by using the present form of the verb *have* or *be* with the past participle of the main verb. Examples include *have mopped* and *is given*.

Present Perfect Formation of Have

Person	Subject	Verb Formation
First	I	have said
Second	you	have said
Third	he, she, it	has said
Second (plural)	you	have said
Third (plural)	they, we	have said

Present Perfect Formation of Be

Person	Subject	Verb Formation
First	I	am shocked
Second	you	are shocked
Third	he, she, it	is shocked
Second (plural)	you	are shocked
Third (plural)	they, we	are shocked

The Present Perfect Tense of Jamaican Creole

In the present perfect tense of Jamaican Creole, main verbs used with *ha* (E. *have*) are used differently than main verbs used with *bi* (E. *be*). The verb *ha* is omitted, and the main verb is used in its base infinitive form. There are words (usually adverbs) that give the reader or listener an idea about when the action occurred (e.g., *now, already*).

> When the main verb is accompanied by another verb, this verb is called a **helping verb**. An example of a main verb and a helping verb combination is *have seen*. In the example, *see* is the main verb, and *have* is the helping verb.

Present Perfect Formation of Seh

Person	Subject	Verb Formation	English Meaning
First	mi	seh	have said
Second	yuh	seh	have said
Third	im, shi, ih/it	seh	has said
Second (plural)	unnu	seh	have said
Third (plural)	dem, wi	seh	have said

Here are some examples of the past perfect tense with the verb *have*:

Jamaican Creole	English
Deeh <u>iht</u> six apple areddi.	lit. They <u>eat</u> six apples already. (*They have eaten six apples already.*)
June <u>pyeh</u> di money long time agoh.	lit. June <u>pay</u> the money [a] long time ago. (*June has paid the money [a] long time ago.*)
Shi <u>goh</u> deh bifuo.	lit. She <u>goes</u> there before. (*She has gone there before.*)

When the verb *bi* (E. *be*) acts as the helping verb, *bi* is omitted since the past participle of the main verb acts like an adjective, and the verb is omitted before adjectives. Examples of this include:

Person	Subject	Verb Formation	English Meaning
First	mi	shock	am shocked
Second	yuh	shock	are shocked
Third	im, shi, ih/it	shock	is shocked
Second (plural)	unnu	shock	are shocked
Third (plural)	dem, wi	shock	are shocked

Here are some examples of Jamaican Creole sentences with their English meaning:

Jamaican Creole	English
Di mango <u>iht</u>.	lit. The mango <u>eat</u>.
	(*The mango is eaten*.)
Shoes <u>sell</u> inna di store.	lit. Shoes <u>sell</u> in the store.
	(*Shoes are sold in the store*.)
Andre <u>prepare</u>.	lit. Andre <u>prepare</u>.
	(*Andre is prepared*.)

When the Verb Bi is the Main Verb

In the present perfect tense, the speaker can choose to form the sentence in two ways when *bi* is the main verb. These are discussed below.

Instance One

The verb can be formed like the present tense (review if necessary). An adverb or phrase indicating that the action took place in the past and continues to the present is necessary to make the meaning clear. For example:

Jamaican Creole	English
Shi <u>deh</u> ya frau yessideh.	lit. She <u>is</u> here from yesterday.
	(*She has been here from yesterday.*)
Mi <u>a</u> di principal one iyer now.	lit. I <u>am</u> the principal one year now.
	(*I have been the principal for one year now.*)
Benny <u>a</u> mi fren since high school.	lit. Benny <u>is</u> my friend since high school.
	(*Benny has been my friend since high school.*)

In the previous examples, *yessideh*, *one year now*, and *since high school* tell us when the events started. They all began at some time in the past and continue to the present.

Instance Two

The verb can be formed like the English present perfect tense that uses E. *been*. The verb *have* that comes before the past participle of the main verb *be* in English is omitted in Jamaican Creole. For example:

Jamaican Creole	English
Mi madda <u>been</u> tired.	lit. My mother <u>been</u> tired.
	(*My mother has been tired.*)
Mi <u>been</u> at di shop.	lit. I <u>been</u> at the shop.
	(*I have been at the shop.*)
Wi <u>been</u> expecting it.	lit. We <u>been</u> expecting it.
	(*We have been expecting it.*)

The Verb Goh In the Present Perfect Tense

The verb *goh* (E. *go*) is one of two irregular verbs in the present perfect tense. Its formation is similar to the English formation. The same past participle (E. *gone*) is used in Jamaican Creole, but the verb *ha* and *bi* are omitted. For example:

Jamaican Creole	English
Henry <u>gone</u>.	lit. Henry <u>gone</u>.
	(*Henry is gone.*)
Wi <u>gone</u> huom.	lit. We <u>gone</u> home.
	(*We have gone home.*)
Di pikini <u>gone</u> a shop.	lit. The child <u>gone</u> to shop.
	(*The child has gone to the shop.*)
Mi <u>gone</u>.	lit. I <u>gone</u>.
	(*I am gone.*)

The Verb Duh In the Present Perfect Tense

The verb *duh* (E. *do*) is irregular in the present perfect tense when the verb *bi* is used before it. Its formation is similar to the English formation. The same past participle (E. *done*) is used in Jamaican Creole, but the verb *be* that comes before *done* in English is omitted in Jamaican Creole. For example:

Jamaican Creole	English
Di employee <u>done</u> wid di job.	lit. The employee <u>done</u> with the job.
	(*The employee is done with the job.*)
Deeh <u>done</u> meet.	lit. They <u>done</u> meet.
	(*They are done meeting.*)
Shi <u>done</u> wid di book.	lit. Shi <u>done</u> with the book.
	(*Shi is done with the book.*)

When *duh* is used with the verb *ha*, the verb *duh* behaves like a regular verb and is formed like the Jamaican Creole present tense. The verb *ha* is omitted in Jamaican Creole. For example:

Jamaican Creole	English
Shane <u>duh</u> im wok areddi.	lit. Shane <u>do</u> his work already.
	(*Shane has done his work already.*)
Mi <u>duh</u> five math problem.	lit. I <u>do</u> five math problem.
	(*I have done five math problems.*)

Jamaican Creole	English
Di pikini <u>duh</u> aar family proud.	lit. The child <u>does</u> her family proud.
	(The child has done her family proud.)

The Continuous Present Perfect Tense

The Continuous Present Perfect Tense of English

The continuous present perfect tense tells us about an action that happened for a period of time in the past and continues to the present moment. In English, it is formed by placing *has been* or *have been* before the main verb ending in –ing.

Person	Subject	Verb Formation
First	I	have been telling
Second	you	have been feeling
Third	he, she, it	has been asking
Second (plural)	you	have been doing
Third (plural)	they, we	have been reading

The Continuous Present Perfect Tense of Jamaican Creole

In Jamaican Creole, the continuous present perfect tense is not used. The simple present tense or the continuous present tense is used in place of the continuous present perfect tense. When the simple present tense is used, the speaker lets the listener know how long the action has been going on for up until the present.

Person	Subject	Instead of Saying in English:	Subject	One Would Say in Jamaican Creole:
First	I	have been telling	mi	tell
Second	you	have have been feeling	yuh	feel

Person	Subject	Instead of Saying in English:	Subject	One Would Say in Jamaican Creole:
Third	he, she, it	has been asking	im, shi, ih/it	aks
Second (plural)	you	have been doing	unnu	duh
Third (plural)	they, we	have been reading	dem, wi	read

For example:

Jamaican Creole: James <u>wok</u> a Kingston fi <u>iyerz now</u>.

English: lit. James <u>work</u> in Kingston for <u>years now</u>.

(*James has been working in Kingston for years now.*)

In other cases where the speaker does not say how long the action has been going on for, the continuous present tense is used.

Person	Subject	Instead of Saying in English:	Subject	One Would Say in Jamaican Creole:
First	I	have been telling	mi	a tell
Second	you	have have been feeling	yuh	a feel
Third	he, she, it	has been asking	im, shi, ih/it	a aks
Second (plural)	you	have been doing	unnu	a duh
Third (plural)	they, we	have been reading	dem, wi	a read

Example of the Jamaican Creole continuous present perfect tense:

Jamaican Creole: Di girl <u>a plyeh</u> wid aar fren inna di yaad.

English: lit. The girl <u>is playing</u> with her friend in the yard.

(*The girl has been playing with her friend in the yard.*)

Less frequently, a form of the English continuous present perfect tense is used in Jamaican Creole. The verb *have* that is used in English is omitted in Jamaican Creole. The English verb *be* along with the present participle of the main verb ending in *–ing* are used.

Person	Subject	Instead of Saying in English:	Subject	One Would Say in Jamaican Creole:
First	I	have been telling	mi	been telling
Second	you	have have been feeling	yuh	been feeling
Third	he, she, it	has been asking	im, shi, ih/it	been aks-in
Second (plural)	you	have been doing	unnu	been duh-in
Third (plural)	they, we	have been reading	dem, wi	been reading

For the purpose of distinguishing between the English form and the Jamaican Creole form of a verb, -in is used instead of –ing for Jamaican Creole verbs (e.g., *duh-in* (E. *doing*).

For example:

Jamaican Creole: Mi <u>been duh-in</u> well inna school.

English: I <u>have been doing</u> well in school.

Practice Exercise 44

Translate the following sentences to English. The verb should be in the present perfect or the continuous present perfect tense.

1. ᴶMi ᴶsi him every time ᴶim come ᴶa ᴶdi meeting.

_____

2. Mi fren ᴱfinish ᴱpacking aar ᴱbook dem inna aar ᴱbag.

_____

3. Di ᴱstudent duh ᴱwell inna di ᴱexam.

   _____

4. ᴶDem been cleaning ᴶdi house frau ᴶmaanin.

   _____

5. Mi faada ᴱdone wid ᴱcleaning ᴱup di gyaabij inna di yaad.

   _____

6. Hanna been to ᴶdi city a lot ᴶwid ᴶaar ᴶmadda.

   _____

7. Mi ᴱbeen dyer.

   _____

8. ᴱKenroy seh im naah goh wid wi.

   _____

9. ᴶWi ᴶa pack ᴶfi ᴶwi trip from long time.

   _____

10. Mi ᴱuncle a ᴱdrive tracta fi iyerz ᴱnow.

   _____

Practice Exercise 45

Translate the following sentences to Jamaican Creole. Use any adverb or adverb phrase you think might help make the meaning of the sentence clearer.

1. Peter-Gaye has played the game with her brother.

   _____

2. We have been giving them money for months.

   _____

3. Gina has washed the dishes.

   _____

4. The student has been leaving her textbooks in the classroom.

    _____

5. The tap has been running for ten minutes.

    _____

6. The children have played with the toys.

    _____

7. My mother has been buying groceries at the store.

    _____

8. The radio has been playing on the same station for thirty minutes now.

    _____

9. Henry has applied for the scholarship.

    _____

10. We have been going to the same restaurant every week.

    _____

Practice Exercise 46

Fill in the blanks with the correct Jamaican Creole form of the verbs in brackets. Verbs should be formed in the present perfect tense.

1. ᴱJenny _____ mi seh shi aggo goh spen ᴱtime wid aar anti inna ᴱMontego ᴱBay. (tell)

2. Di tiicha _____ di pikini dem fi styeh bihain afta ᴱclass tudeh. (aks)

3. Shi _____ dat shi aggo bi ᴱretiring a di en a di iyer. (announce)

4. Dem neva baan inna ᴱKingston, ᴱbut deeh _____ deh fi wau ᴱlong ᴱtime ᴱnow. (live)

5. ᴱTwice tudeh, wi _____ inna ᴱeach adda. (run)

6. Jeffery ᴶauh Jaden ＿＿＿＿＿＿＿ Pam ᴶa leave ᴶdi ᴶlaibri ᴶwid new textbooks. (si)

7. ᴶWi ＿＿＿＿＿＿＿ ᴶa Addis Ababa. (bi)

8. ᴶDi notice ＿＿＿＿＿＿＿ to ᴶdi wall. (styep'l)

9. Aalduo di ᴱsun ＿＿＿＿＿＿＿, ih did ᴱchilly. (rise)

10. ᴱKim ＿＿＿＿＿＿＿ ᴱall aar ᴱclothes dem an ᴱput dem inna di ᴱcloset. (fuol)

Practice Exercise 47

Fill in the blanks with the correct form of the verbs in brackets. Verbs should be used in the forms of the continuous present perfect tense used in Jamaican Creole.

1. Di byebi ＿＿＿＿＿＿＿ fi ᴱgrab di bakk'l weh sidong pan ᴱtop a di tyeb'l. (try)

2. ᴱKenny ᴱunsure bout ᴱhow fi ᴱcomplete im ᴱassignment, ᴱbut im ＿＿＿＿＿＿＿ pan ih fi wau ᴱhour ᴱnow. (wok)

3. Di ᴱman ＿＿＿＿＿＿＿ ᴱgrass frau di gyaad'n an ＿＿＿＿＿＿＿ flowaz. (pull, plant)

4. Di pyenta ＿＿＿＿＿＿＿ di ᴱhouse ᴱblue an ᴱpurple. (pyent)

5. Di ᴱtenant complyen ᴱto di lanlaad seh ᴱfew ᴱsheet a ᴱzinc ＿＿＿＿＿＿＿ frau di ᴱroof. (fall)

6. Mi granmadda ＿＿＿＿＿＿＿ wau ᴱvideo pan aar ᴱnew fuon. (watch)

7. ᴶDi ᴶcompuuta ᴶbrok, ᴶsoh Julia ＿＿＿＿＿＿＿ ᴶaar assignment by writing it. (complete)

8. Shi ＿＿＿＿＿＿＿ fi hyeh ᴱfrom aar fren tudeh. (expek)

9. ᴱGregory ＿＿＿＿＿＿＿ di ᴱfloor ᴱwhile im sista ＿＿＿＿＿＿＿ di ᴱdishes dem. (clean, wash)

10. Ih ＿＿＿＿＿＿＿ ᴱall dyeh. (ryen)

Practice Exercise 48

Determine whether the underlined verbs in the following sentences are in the present perfect tense or the continuous present perfect tense. Write your answer on the line.

1. He <u>has been ordered</u> by the court to pay a fine for being disruptive in the courtroom.

    _____

2. Jeremy <u>has been writing</u> an essay so that he can enter the competition.

    _____

3. It <u>has been decided</u> that fares will increase at the end of the year.

    _____

4. I <u>have eaten</u> my lunch already.

    _____

5. Marcia likes to dance, so she <u>has been taking</u> dance lessons.

    _____

6. The benches <u>have been painted</u> to protect them from the rain.

    _____

7. The plumber <u>has been taking</u> a long time to fix the pipe.

    _____

8. My mother is concerned that the seal on the bottle <u>is broken.</u>

    _____

9. We <u>have finished unpacking</u> the furniture from the truck.

    _____

10. The dog <u>has been sitting</u> on the stairs for a long while.

    _____

Practice Exercise 49

Use the following words to form sentences in one form of the continuous present perfect tense of Jamaican Creole. Identify the part of speech of the word you used by writing it on the line (e.g. noun, verb, etc.).

baak *n., v.* bark

cratch *n., v.* scratch

dashweh *v. phrase* throw away; spill

gaa *contr.* go to

paach *v.* parch

ragga-ragga *adj., v.* untidy (regarding clothes) (regards clothing)

ton *n., v.* turn

1. _____

   Part of speech _____

2. _____

   Part of speech _____

3. _____

   Part of speech _____

4. _____

   Part of speech _____

5. _____

   Part of speech _____

6. _____

   Part of speech _____

7. _____

   Part of speech _____

The Past Perfect Tense

The Past Perfect Tense of English

The past perfect tense of English is formed by using the past tense of the verb *have* or *be* with the past participle of the main verb. It describes actions that began and ended in the past. Examples include *had mopped* and *was given*.

Present Perfect Formation with Have

Person	Subject	Verb Formation
First	I	had said
Second	you	had said
Third	he, she, it	had said
Second (plural)	you	had said
Third (plural)	they, we	had said

Present Perfect Formation with Be

Person	Subject	Verb Formation
First	I	was shocked
Second	you	were shocked
Third	he, she, it	was shocked

Person	Subject	Verb Formation
Second (plural)	you	were shocked
Third (plural)	they, we	were shocked

The Past Perfect Tense of Jamaican Creole

In Jamaican Creole, the past perfect tense is formed by using *did* (also used as *beeh, weeh, beeh did,* or *weeh did*) along with the base infinitive form of the verb. This is also one of the formations used in the simple past tense as discussed previously.

When the Past Perfect Tense is Formed with Did

Person	Subject	Verb Formation	English Meaning
First	mi	did run	had run
Second	yuh	did study	had studied
Third	im, shi, ih/it	did plyeh	had played
Second (plural)	unnu	did read	had read
Third (plural)	dem, wi	did duh	had done

When the Past Perfect Tense is Formed with Beeh

Person	Subject	Verb Formation	English Meaning
First	mi	beeh run	had run
Second	yuh	beeh study	had studied
Third	im, shi, ih/it	beeh plyeh	had played
Second (plural)	unnu	beeh read	had read
Third (plural)	dem, wi	beeh duh	had done

When the Past Perfect Tense is Formed with Weeh

Person	Subject	Verb Formation	English Meaning
First	mi	weeh run	had run

Person	Subject	Verb Formation	English Meaning
Second	yuh	weeh study	had studied
Third	im, shi, ih/it	weeh plyeh	had played
Second (plural)	unnu	weeh read	had read
Third (plural)	dem, wi	weeh duh	had done

When the Past Perfect Tense is Formed with Beeh Did

Person	Subject	Verb Formation	English Meaning
First	mi	beeh did run	had run
Second	yuh	beeh did study	had studied
Third	im, shi, ih/it	beeh did plyeh	had played
Second (plural)	unnu	beeh did read	had read
Third (plural)	dem, wi	beeh did duh	had done

When the Past Perfect Tense is Formed with Weeh Did

Person	Subject	Verb Formation	English Meaning
First	mi	weeh did run	had run
Second	yuh	weeh did study	had studied
Third	im, shi, ih/it	weeh did plyeh	had played
Second (plural)	unnu	weeh did read	had read
Third (plural)	dem, wi	weeh did duh	had done

The following sentences are examples of the past perfect tense:

Jamaican Creole	English
Jim <u>did gi</u> aar di TV.	Jim <u>had given</u> her the TV.
Iih <u>weeh pick</u> up sooh fren pan di wyeh huom.	He <u>had picked</u> up some friends on the way home.
Ian <u>beeh did put</u> five dalla inna di piggybank.	Ian <u>had put</u> five dollars in the piggybank.

The Verb Bi In the Past Perfect Tense

In the past perfect tense, the verb *bi* (E. *be*) is formed as it is in the simple past tense (review if necessary). For example:

Jamaican Creole	English
Mi <u>did deh</u> a wok when im lef.	I <u>had been</u> at work when he left.
Di pikini <u>beeh did</u> upset seh aar madda <u>beeh did</u> absent fi di shuo.	The child <u>had been</u> upset that her mother <u>had been</u> absent for the show.
Suzie <u>wen a</u> di laas one fi reach huom.	Suzie <u>had been</u> the last one to reach home.

The Verb Goh In the Past Perfect Tense

In the past perfect tense, the regular formation of the verb *goh* (E. *go*) is *did goh* (also used as *beeh goh*, *weeh goh*, *beeh did goh*, or *weeh did goh*).

The Use of Goh

When Goh is Used with Did

Person	Subject	Verb Formation	English Meaning
First	mi	did goh	had gone
Second	yuh	did goh	had gone
Third	im, shi, ih/it	did goh	had gone
Second (plural)	unnu	did goh	had gone
Third (plural)	dem, wi	did goh	had gone

When Goh is Used with Beeh

Person	Subject	Verb Formation	English Meaning
First	mi	beeh goh	had gone
Second	yuh	beeh goh	had gone

Person	Subject	Verb Formation	English Meaning
Third	im, shi, ih/it	beeh goh	had gone
Second (plural)	unnu	beeh goh	had gone
Third (plural)	dem, wi	beeh goh	had gone

When Goh is Used with Weeh

Person	Subject	Verb Formation	English Meaning
First	mi	weeh goh	had gone
Second	yuh	weeh goh	had gone
Third	im, shi, ih/it	weeh goh	had gone
Second (plural)	unnu	weeh goh	had gone
Third (plural)	dem, wi	weeh goh	had gone

When Goh is Used with Beeh Did

Person	Subject	Verb Formation	English Meaning
First	mi	beeh did goh	had gone
Second	yuh	beeh did goh	had gone
Third	im, shi, ih/it	beeh did goh	had gone
Second (plural)	unnu	beeh did goh	had gone
Third (plural)	dem, wi	beeh did goh	had gone

When Goh is Used with Weeh Did

Person	Subject	Verb Formation	English Meaning
First	mi	weeh did goh	had gone
Second	yuh	weeh did goh	had gone
Third	im, shi, ih/it	weeh did goh	had gone
Second (plural)	unnu	weeh did goh	had gone
Third (plural)	dem, wi	weeh did goh	had gone

The following sentences are examples of the use of *goh* in the past perfect tense:

Jamaican Creole	English
Susan <u>did goh</u> a Browns Town laas week.	Susan <u>had gone</u> to Browns Town last week.
Mi <u>weeh goh</u> deh wid mi faada an bredda.	I <u>had gone</u> there with my father and brother.
Erica <u>beeh did goh</u> a di museum.	Erica <u>had gone</u> to the museum.

The Use of Gone

If one is describing that an event or action happened while someone was on their way to some place, the English participle *gone* is most often used along with *did* (or *beeh, weeh, beeh did,* or *weeh did*). *Gone* is also used if the action or event happened shortly after the person left.

When Gone is Used with Did

Person	Subject	Verb Formation	English Meaning
First	mi	did gone	had gone
Second	yuh	did gone	had gone
Third	im, shi, ih/it	did gone	had gone
Second (plural)	unnu	did gone	had gone
Third (plural)	dem, wi	did gone	had gone

When Gone is Used with Beeh

Person	Subject	Verb Formation	English Meaning
First	mi	beeh gone	had gone
Second	yuh	beeh gone	had gone
Third	im, shi, ih/it	beeh gone	had gone
Second (plural)	unnu	beeh gone	had gone
Third (plural)	dem, wi	beeh gone	had gone

When Gone is Used with Weeh

Person	Subject	Verb Formation	English Meaning
First	mi	weeh gone	had gone
Second	yuh	weeh gone	had gone
Third	im, shi, ih/it	weeh gone	had gone
Second (plural)	unnu	weeh gone	had gone
Third (plural)	dem, wi	weeh gone	had gone

When Gone is Used with Beeh Did

Person	Subject	Verb Formation	English Meaning
First	mi	beeh did gone	had gone
Second	yuh	beeh did gone	had gone
Third	im, shi, ih/it	beeh did gone	had gone
Second (plural)	unnu	beeh did gone	had gone
Third (plural)	dem, wi	beeh did gone	had gone

When Gone is Used with Weeh Did

Person	Subject	Verb Formation	English Meaning
First	mi	weeh did gone	had gone
Second	yuh	weeh did gone	had gone
Third	im, shi, ih/it	weeh did gone	had gone
Second (plural)	unnu	weeh did gone	had gone
Third (plural)	dem, wi	weeh did gone	had gone

The following sentences are examples of the use of *goh* in the past perfect tense:

Jamaican Creole	English
Sam did gone a town when im family lef.	Sam had gone to town when his family left.

Jamaican Creole	English
Wi <u>weeh gone</u> huom afta wi win di prize.	We <u>had gone</u> home after we won the prize.
Tim <u>beeh did gone</u> a grong when yuh call.	Tim <u>had gone</u> to [the] field when you called.

The Continuous Past Perfect Tense

The Continuous Past Perfect Tense of English

The continuous past perfect tense tells us what went on for a period of time in the past before coming to an end. The table below shows some examples of the continuous past perfect tense of English:

Person	Subject	Verb Formation
First	I	had been playing
Second	you	had been seeing
Third	he, she, it	had been allowing
Second (plural)	you	had been telling
Third (plural)	they, we	had been working

The Continuous Past Perfect Tense of Jamaican Creole

In Jamaican Creole, the continuous past perfect tense is formed like the continuous past tense. *Did a* (also used as *ben a, wen a, did deh, beeh deh, weeh deh, beeh did deh*, or *weeh did deh*) is used before the base infinitive form of the verb.

When the Continuous Past Perfect Tense is Formed with Did A

Person	Subject	Verb Formation	English Meaning
First	mi	did a run	had been running
Second	yuh	did a study	had been studying

Person	Subject	Verb Formation	English Meaning
Third	im, shi, ih/it	did a plyeh	had been playing
Second (plural)	unnu	did a read	had been reading
Third (plural)	dem, wi	did a duh	had been doing

When the Continuous Past Perfect Tense is Formed with Ben A

Person	Subject	Verb Formation	English Meaning
First	mi	ben a run	had been running
Second	yuh	ben a study	had been studying
Third	im, shi, ih/it	ben a plyeh	had been playing
Second (plural)	unnu	ben a read	had been reading
Third (plural)	dem, wi	ben a duh	had been doing

When the Continuous Past Perfect Tense is Formed with Wen A

Person	Subject	Verb Formation	English Meaning
First	mi	wen a run	had been running
Second	yuh	wen a study	had been studying
Third	im, shi, ih/it	wen a plyeh	had been playing
Second (plural)	unnu	wen a read	had been reading
Third (plural)	dem, wi	wen a duh	had been doing

When the Continuous Past Perfect Tense is Formed with Did Deh

Person	Subject	Verb Formation	English Meaning
First	mi	did deh run	had been running
Second	yuh	did deh study	had been studying
Third	im, shi, ih/it	did deh plyeh	had been playing
Second (plural)	unnu	did deh read	had been reading
Third (plural)	dem, wi	did deh duh	had been doing

When the Continuous Past Perfect Tense is Formed with Beeh Deh

Person	Subject	Verb Formation	English Meaning
First	mi	beeh deh run	had been running
Second	yuh	beeh deh study	had been studying
Third	im, shi, ih/it	beeh deh plyeh	had been playing
Second (plural)	unnu	beeh deh read	had been reading
Third (plural)	dem, wi	beeh deh duh	had been doing

When the Continuous Past Perfect Tense is Formed with Weeh Deh

Person	Subject	Verb Formation	English Meaning
First	mi	weeh deh run	had been running
Second	yuh	weeh deh study	had been studying
Third	im, shi, ih/it	weeh deh plyeh	had been playing
Second (plural)	unnu	weeh deh read	had been reading
Third (plural)	dem, wi	weeh deh duh	had been doing

When the Continuous Past Perfect Tense is Formed with Beeh Did Deh

Person	Subject	Verb Formation	English Meaning
First	mi	beeh did deh run	had been running
Second	yuh	beeh did deh study	had been studying
Third	im, shi, ih/it	beeh did deh plyeh	had been playing
Second (plural)	unnu	beeh did deh read	had been reading
Third (plural)	dem, wi	beeh did deh duh	had been doing

When the Continuous Past Perfect Tense is Formed with Weeh Did Deh

Person	Subject	Verb Formation	English Meaning
First	mi	weeh did deh run	had been running
Second	yuh	weeh did deh study	had been studying
Third	im, shi, ih/it	weeh did deh plyeh	had been playing
Second (plural)	unnu	weeh did deh read	had been reading
Third (plural)	dem, wi	weeh did deh duh	had been doing

The following sentences are examples of the continuous past perfect tense:

Jamaican Creole	English
Lorna <u>did a kuom</u> aar hyer.	Lorna <u>had been combing</u> her hair.
Dina <u>beeh did deh cook</u> rice and peas.	Dina <u>had been cooking</u> rice and peas.
Mi <u>weeh deh look</u> fi mi shoes dem inna di closet.	I <u>had been looking</u> for my shoes in the closet.

Practice Exercise 50

Translate the following sentences to the past perfect tense of English.

1. Winston ᴶdid buy ᴶwau new house.

   _____

2. ᴱNicoya beeh gi aar wau ᴱnew ᴱdress fi ᴱwear goh a di paati.

   _____

3. Di gyaadna weeh did deh ya ᴱall dyeh.

   _____

4. Aalduo mi madda inna wau ᴱgood ᴱmood ᴱnow, shi did ᴱupset yessideh.

   _____

5. Di ^Edetective weeh ^Esolve di kyes.

_____

6. Wi beeh did lef ^Eout fi di ^Eairport ^Etwo owa bifuo wi beeh did ^Eschedule fi ^Eleave.

_____

7. Di ^Ewall beeh ^Efall afta nof iyer.

_____

8. Mi an mi bredda did uopen wau ^Enew ^Eaccount a di ^Ebank inna ^Etown.

_____

9. ^EZaria did spen wau ^Eweek inna ^EGhana pan vekyeshan.

_____

10. Dem did deh a di ^Ebeach, ^Eeven duo dem seh dem did deh a wok.

_____

Practice Exercise 51

Translate the following sentences to Jamaican Creole.

1. They had been watching the game in the living room.

_____

2. Janice had been doing her best to keep her business open.

_____

3. The boys had been playing football on the field when the lightening struck.

_____

4. The handyman had been painting the walls in the kitchen.

_____

5. I had been writing a story.

_____

6. The men had been rafting on the river even though it had been raining.

_____

7. The workmen had been paving the roads, so we had to find another route.

_____

8. Demar had been decorating the room with dark colors.

_____

9. Things had been flowing smoothly since we hired an extra worker for the job.

_____

10. Schools had been closing early.

_____

Practice Exercise 52

Translate the following sentences to the past perfect tense of English, and underline the verbs in the past perfect tense.

1. Bianca ᴶbeeh did run up ᴶdi hill.

_____

2. ᴱSherry-Ann did tek wau ᴱlong ᴱtime fi ᴱfinish aar projek.

_____

3. Dem weeh wok pan di ᴱresearch fi iyerz.

_____

4. Mi bredda did ᴱput di pikcha pan di ᴱwall, ᴱbut ih beeh ᴱfall ᴱoff.

_____

5. Di pikini dem beeh did ᴱput di cluoz inna di baaskit.

_____

6. ᴱHurricane weeh did distraah ᴱhalf a di ᴱtown.

_____

7. Di likk'l bwuay beeh iht ᴱall a di ᴱice-cream inna di ᴱbowl.

_____

8. Di faama dem weeh ᴱplough di fiil fi ᴱplant di ᴱnew ᴱcrop.

_____

9. ᴶDi ᴶtiicha did complete ᴶdi lesson early.

_____

10. Wi did ᴱtell dem seh wi noh expek dem fi bi dyer.

_____

Practice Exercise 53

Translate the following sentences to the continuous past perfect tense of English, and underline the verbs in the continuous past perfect tense.

1. Mi finga beeh did a ᴱhurt mi.

_____

2. ᴱSix diffrent ᴱmovie weeh did a shuo inna di tyeta.

_____

3. Di ᴱgirl dem beeh did deh plyeh ᴱhopscotch ᴱout inna di school₁yaad.

_____

4. Di ᴱstore did a opin lyet ᴱevery dyeh.

_____

5. Di ᴱsun weeh did a ᴱset oova di ᴱhill.

_____

6. Wi beeh did deh ᴱget ᴱlesson afta ᴱschool fi ᴱhelp wi wid wi ᴱmaths ᴱskills.

_____

7. ^EDanny beeh did a ^Eget ^Eangry wid im fren.

_____

8. Mi faada did deh ^Eiron mi yunifaam fi goh a ^Eschool ^Etomorrow.

_____

9. ^EAll a di ^Echicken dem inna di kub weeh did deh ^Ecackle.

_____

10. Dem did ^Ja travel ^Jfi miles ^Jfi get ^Jdyer.

_____

Practice Exercise 54

Fill in the blanks with the appropriate verb in either the past perfect or continuous past perfect tense to complete each sentence.

1. Di ^Ecat _____ afta di ^Echicken.

2. Di higla _____ inna wau ^Estall pan di ^Eside a di ruod.

3. Mi _____ dinna ^Ewhen mi hyeh di ^Enews.

4. Henry _____ ^Jfi ^Jdi exam, but Sheena _____ ^Jfiar exam.

5. Di ryedio _____ ^Eoff di tyeb'l an mash-op.

6. Di ^Ecaptain a di ^Ecricket ^Eteam _____ di ^Eprize fi muos ^Eoutstanding pleya.

7. Kenroy _____ new sheet ^Jpan ^Jdi bed.

8. Iiv'n duo ^EDiane neva did goh wid wi, wi ^Estill _____ ^Efun.

9. Di ruod frau mi ^Euncle ^Ehouse ^Eto mi granmadda ^Ehouse _____.

10. ^JDi coffee _____.

Practice Exercise 55

Use the following words to form sentences in either the past perfect or continuous past perfect tense of Jamaican Creole. Identify the part of speech of the word you used by writing it on the line (e.g. noun, verb, etc.).

aalduo *conj.* although　　　**kowl** *adj., n.* cold
dyersoh *adv., n.* there　　　**mek** *v.* let; make; allow
grii *v. phrase* get along　　**tik** *n., v.* stick
ha *v.* have

1. _____

　　Part of speech _____
2. _____

　　Part of speech _____
3. _____

　　Part of speech _____
4. _____

　　Part of speech _____
5. _____

　　Part of speech _____
6. _____

　　Part of speech _____
7. _____

　　Part of speech _____

The Future Tense

The Future Tense of English

The future tense lets us know what is going to happen. An example of the future tense of English is *will have*. Here are some verbs in the future tense of English:

Person	Subject	Verb Formation
First	I	will send
Second	you	will take
Third	he, she, it	will swim
Second (plural)	you	will explain
Third (plural)	they, we	will allow

The Future Tense of Jamaican Creole

In Jamaican Creole, the future tense is formed in two ways:

1. By placing the auxiliary verb *a goh* (also used as *ooh* or *aggo*) before the base infinitive form of the main verb to indicate that the action or event is going to occur in the future. *A goh* means *will, is going to,* or *are going to*.

> An **auxiliary verb** is used before a main verb to modify its meaning in some way (for example, *will* is the auxiliary verb in the verb phrase *will go*).

When the Future Tense Formed with A Goh

Person	Subject	Verb Formation	English Meaning
First	mi	a goh si	will/is going to see
Second	yuh	a goh goh	will/is going to go
Third	im, shi, ih/it	a goh tell	will/is going to tell
Second (plural)	unnu	a goh travel	will/is going to travel
Third (plural)	dem, wi	a goh climb	will/is going to climb

When the Future Tense Formed with Ooh

Person	Subject	Verb Formation	English Meaning
First	mi	ooh si	will/is going to see
Second	yuh	ooh goh	will/is going to go
Third	im, shi, ih/it	ooh tell	will/is going to tell
Second (plural)	unnu	ooh travel	will/is going to travel
Third (plural)	dem, wi	ooh climb	will/is going to climb

When the Future Tense Formed with Aggo

Person	Subject	Verb Formation	English Meaning
First	mi	aggo si	will/is going to see
Second	yuh	aggo goh	will/is going to go
Third	im, shi, ih/it	aggo tell	will/is going to tell
Second (plural)	unnu	aggo travel	will/is going to travel
Third (plural)	dem, wi	aggo climb	will/is going to climb

The following sentences are examples of the future tense when formed with *a goh, ooh*, or *aggo*:

Jamaican Creole	English
Wi <u>a goh travel</u> inna June.	We <u>are going to travel</u> in June.
Ryen <u>aggo fall</u> tudeh.	Rain <u>is going to fall</u> today.
*Pete <u>ooh siim</u> when im goh a di meeting.	Pete <u>is going to see him</u> when he goes to the meeting.

Si and im are usually pronounced as one word (siim).

2. By placing the auxiliary verb *gweeh* before the base infinitive form of the verb to mean *will, is going to*, or *are going to*.

When the Future Tense is Formed with Gweeh

Person	Subject	Verb Formation	English Meaning
First	mi	gweeh si	will/is going to see
Second	yuh	gweeh goh	will/is going to go
Third	im, shi, ih/it	gweeh tell	will/is going to tell
Second (plural)	unnu	gweeh travel	will/is going to travel
Third (plural)	dem, wi	gweeh climb	will/is going to climb

The following sentences are examples of the future tense that is formed with *gweeh*:

Jamaican Creole	English
Dem <u>gweeh si</u> wi a di concert.	They <u>will/are going to see</u> us at the concert.
Wi <u>gweeh study</u> inna di maanin.	We <u>will/are going to study</u> in the morning.
Di package <u>gweeh reach</u> soon.	The package <u>will/is going to reach/arrive</u> soon.

The Verb Bi In the Future Tense

In the future tense, the auxiliary verbs *a goh* (*ooh* or *aggo*) and *gweeh* are used before the base infinitive form of the verb *bi* to mean *will be*.

When the Future Tense is Formed with A Goh

Person	Subject	Verb Formation	English Meaning
First	mi	a goh bi	will/is going to be
Second	yuh	a goh bi	will/is going to be
Third	im, shi, ih/it	a goh bi	will/is going to be
Second (plural)	unnu	a goh bi	will/is going to be
Third (plural)	dem, wi	a goh bi	will/is going to be

When the Future Tense is Formed with Gweeh

Person	Subject	Verb Formation	English Meaning
First	mi	gweeh bi	will/is going to be
Second	yuh	gweeh bi	will/is going to be
Third	im, shi, ih/it	gweeh bi	will/is going to be
Second (plural)	unnu	gweeh bi	will/is going to be
Third (plural)	dem, wi	gweeh bi	will/is going to be

The following are examples of the verb *bi* in the future tense:

Jamaican Creole	English
Shi <u>aggo bi</u> twenty soon.	She <u>will be</u> twenty soon.
Di cat <u>aggo bi</u> sick if ih iht nof food.	The cat <u>will be</u> sick if it eats a lot [of] food.
Dem <u>gweeh bi</u> inna di store craas di ruod.	They <u>will be</u> in the store across the road.

When the Verb Bi is Used with Adjectives

Sometimes, the main verb is omitted before adjectives. *A goh* (*ooh* or *aggo*) or *gweeh* is still used before the adjective. For example:

Jamaican Creole	English
Di food <u>aggo tyesti</u>.	The food <u>is going [to be] tasty</u>.
Mi sista <u>gweeh upset</u>.	My sister <u>is going [to be] upset</u>.
Kevin <u>aggo excited</u> fi si yuh.	Kevin <u>will [be] excited</u> to see you.

When an adverb occurs between the verb or verb phrase and the adjective, however, the base infinitive form *bi* is often used after *aggo, ooh,* and *gweeh*. For example:

Jamaican Creole	English
Denisha <u>aggo bi soh taiyad</u>.	Denisha <u>is going to be so tired</u>.
Shi <u>gweeh bi very happy</u>.	She <u>is going to be very happy</u>.
Di fruit dem <u>aggo likely bi fine</u> afta a few dyeh.	The fruits <u>are likely going to be fine</u> after a few days.

When Bi is Irregular In the Future Tense

The verb *bi* is irregular in the future tense in the following ways:

1. The verb becomes *deh* when used directly before prepositions such as *a* (E. *at*), *pau, (E. on) pan* (E. *on*), *inna* (E. *in*), *oova* (E. *over*), *anda* (E. *under*), etc., and adverbs such as *ya* (E. *here*), *deh* (E. *there*), *dyer* (E. *there*), etc., that state the position or location of the subject. For example:

Jamaican Creole	English
Mi <u>aggo deh a</u> English class soon.	I <u>am going to be at</u> English class soon.
Kadian <u>a goh deh pan</u> di bus.	Kadian <u>is going to be on</u> the bus.
Di box dem <u>aggo deh pan</u> di floor	The boxes <u>are going to be on</u> the floor.

2. Sometimes, the speaker omits the verb before *inna* (E. *in*), *oova* (E. *over*), *anda* (E. *under*), *dong* (E. *down*), *agens* (E. *against*), *afta* (E. *after*), and *aaf* (E. *off*). For example:

Jamaican Creole	English
Di fair <u>gweeh inna</u> di town.	The fair <u>is going [to be] in</u> the town.
Greg <u>aggo dong</u> a di bottom a di hill.	Greg <u>will [be] down</u> at the bottom of the hill.
Mi <u>a goh oova</u> dyer.	I <u>will [be] over</u> there.

Deh is never omitted before the prepositions *a, pan, pau, dyer*, and *ya*. For example:

Jamaican Creole	English
Shi <u>ooh deh a</u> school pau Friday.	She <u>will be at</u> school on Friday.
Di celebrity <u>aggo deh pan</u> di flight.	The celebrity <u>will be on</u> the flight.
Simone <u>gweeh deh ya</u>.	Smone <u>is going to be here</u>.

The Verbs Sidong And Tan-op In the Future Tense

In the future tense, the auxiliary verbs *a goh* (*ooh* or *aggo*) and *gweeh* are used before the base infinitive form of the verbs *sidong and tan-op*.

When the Future Tense is Formed with A Goh

Person	Subject	Verb Formation	English Meaning
First	mi	a goh sidong/ tan-op	will/is going to sit/ stand
Second	yuh	a goh sidong/ tan-op	will/is going to sit/ stand
Third	im, shi, ih/it	a goh sidong/ tan-op	will/is going to sit/ stand
Second (plural)	unnu	a goh sidong/ tan-op	will/is going to sit/ stand

Person	Subject	Verb Formation	English Meaning
Third (plural)	dem, wi	a goh sidong/ tan-op	will/is going to sit/ stand

When the Future Tense is Formed with Gweeh

Person	Subject	Verb Formation	English Meaning
First	mi	gweeh sidong/ tan-op	will/is going to sit/ stand
Second	yuh	gweeh sidong/ tan-op	will/is going to sit/ stand
Third	im, shi, ih/it	gweeh sidong/ tan-op	will/is going to sit/ stand
Second (plural)	unnu	gweeh sidong/ tan-op	will/is going to sit/ stand
Third (plural)	dem, wi	gweeh sidong/ tan-op	will/is going to sit/ stand

The following are examples of the verbs *sidong* and *tan-op* in the future tense:

Jamaican Creole	English
Jim a goh sidong inna di kyaar.	Jim will sit in the car.
Di pikini aggo tan-op inna di hallꞁwyeh.	The child will stand in the hallway.
Dem gweeh sidong till yuh come.	They are going to sit until you come.

When the Verbs Sidong And Tan-op Are Irregular In the Future Tense

When using the verbs *sidong* and *tan-op*, *a* can be used instead of *gweeh* and *a goh* in the future tense.

The following are examples of the verbs *sidong* and *tan-op* when used with *a*:

Jamaican Creole	English
Henry a sidong oova dehsoh till yuh come.	Henry is going to sit over there until you come.
Im a tan-op inna di kaana.	He is going to stand in the corner.
Wi a sidong pan di varanda.	We are going to sit on the veranda.

Suuh And the Future Tense

When *suuh* (E. *soon*) is used before a verb that is formed in the future tense, the auxiliary verbs *a goh* (*ooh* or *aggo*) and *gweeh* are often omitted. You should note that *suuh* is not used before infinitive verbs. E. *Soon* is used before all infinitive verbs (for example, *He is soon to marry*), though Jamaicans rarely use sentences in this format. Examples of the use of *suuh* in the future tense:

Jamaican Creole	English
Mi suuh reach.	lit. I soon reach.
	(*I will soon reach.*)
Shi suuh tek out di gyabij.	lit. She soon take out the garbage.
	(*She will soon take out the garbage.*)
Melissa suuh leave.	lit. Melissa soon leave.
	(*Melissa will soon leave.*)

Note that certain forms of the future tense, such as *will have* and *will have been* are not used in Jamaican Creole.

The Conditional Future Tense

The conditional future tense describes an action or event that might happen in the future and that depends on whether or not another event or action occurs first. It is used in two instances:

1. In the first instance of the conditional future tense, *if* and *when* clauses are used. As described previously, a clause is a phrase with a

subject and a predicate. Examples of the conditional future are *If we leave now, we will make it on time* and *Melissa will see the sign when she is close.* In Jamaican Creole, the conditional future tense also uses *if* and *when* clauses. *Wi* (E. *will*) is used in this instance of the conditional future tense. For example:

Jamaican Creole	English
If wi explyen ih to him, im <u>wi andastan</u>.	If we explain it to him, he <u>will understand</u>.
Im <u>wi si yuh when</u> im reach huom.	He <u>will see you when</u> he reaches home.

In Jamaican Creole, *if* and *when* clauses are not always stated or are not always necessary to state that a condition is present. It is nonetheless understood that the future event is not certain and is based on some unspoken condition. For example:

Jamaican Creole	English
Mi <u>wi si</u> wa mi kyah duh.	I <u>will see</u> what I can do.
Dem <u>wi call</u> yuh.	They <u>will call</u> you.

2. In the second instance of the conditional future tense, the auxiliary verb *would* is used along with an *if* clause. An example of the conditional future tense in the second instance is *If I were to see him, I would tell him*. In Jamaican Creole, *wudda* (E. *would*) is used in this form of the conditional future tense. For example:

Jamaican Creole	English
<u>If</u> im come tudeh, mi <u>wudda</u> get fi siim.	<u>If</u> he comes today, I <u>would</u> get to see him.
Mi <u>wudda</u> goh a di paati <u>if</u> mi did ha company.	I <u>would</u> go to the party <u>if</u> I had company.

In both English and Jamaican Creole, the *if* clause is not always used in the sentence to let you know that a condition exists. In these sentences, another statement would be needed to understand what is happening. For example:

Jamaican Creole	English
Mi madda <u>wudda nuo</u>.	My mother <u>would know</u>.
Shi <u>wudda tell</u> mi.	She <u>would tell</u> me.
Dem <u>wudda andastan</u>.	They <u>would understand</u>.

The Verb Bi In the Conditional Future Tense

The auxiliary verbs *wi* and *wudda* are used before the base infinitive form of the verb *bi* to form the conditional future tense. For example:

Jamaican Creole	English
Dem <u>wi bi</u> dyer if di bus a run.	They <u>will be</u> there if the bus is running.
Letisha <u>wudda bi</u> upset.	Letisha <u>would be</u> upset.
Kemar <u>wi bi</u> hungry if im skip im lunch.	Kemar <u>will be</u> hungry if he skips his lunch.

The verb *bi* can be omitted, and *wi* or *wudda* can be used alone before the adjective, although in some cases *bi* is used. For example:

Jamaican Creole	English
Mi <u>wudda sleepy</u> if mi did styeh up laas night.	I <u>would [be] sleepy</u> if I had stayed up last night.
Di pikini <u>wi fryed</u> if yuh ton off di light.	The child <u>will [be] afraid</u> if you turn off the light.
Mi <u>wi bi glad</u> fi di help.	I <u>will be glad</u> for the help.

When there is an adverb between the verb or verb phrase and the adjective, however, the base infinitive form *bi* is used after *wi* and is not omitted. For example:

Jamaican Creole	English
Im <u>wi bi very happy</u> if yuh goh siim.	He <u>will be very happy</u> if you go [to] see him.
Wi <u>wudda bi soh sad</u> if wi noh get fi goh.	We <u>would be so sad</u> if we did not get to go.

Jamaican Creole	English
Jason <u>wudda likely bi glad</u> fi si yuh.	Jason <u>would likely be glad</u> to see you.

The verb is formed *deh* when used before prepositions such as *a* (E. *at*), *pau* (E. *on*), *pan* (E. *on*), *inna* (E. *in*), *oova* (E. *over*), *anda* (E. *under*), etc., and adverbs such as *ya* (E. *here*), *deh* (E. *there*), *dyer* (E. *there*), etc., that indicate position or location. For example:

Jamaican Creole	English
Mi <u>wudda deh a</u> di mall if mi did ha company.	I <u>would be at</u> the mall if I had company.
Shi <u>wudda deh pan</u> di nex bus.	She <u>would be on</u> the next bus.
Sheena <u>wi deh a</u> Port Antonio tomorrow.	Sheena <u>will (possibly/might) be in</u> Port Antonio tomorrow.

Sometimes speakers of Jamaican Creole omit the verb *bi* before prepositions such as *inna* (E. *in*), *oova* (E. *over*), *anda* (E. *under*), *dong* (E. *down*), *agens* (E. *against*), *afta* (E. *after*), and *aaf* (E. *off*), however. For example:

Jamaican Creole	English
Wi <u>wudda inna</u> di taxi by datdeh time.	We <u>would be in</u> the taxi by that time.
Mi <u>wi inna</u> di store till yuh come.	I <u>will (possibly/might) be in</u> the store until you come.
Im <u>wi oova</u> im cousin house.	He <u>will (possibly/might) be over</u> [at] his cousin's house.

Practice Exercise 56

Translate the following sentences to English.

1. Wi aggo sidong ᴱout inna di ᴱsun fi ᴱten ᴱminutes.
2. Shi wi ᴱlook fi di ᴱbook afta shi ᴱfinish aar huomwok.
3. ᴱIf ᴱGavina did ha ᴱmoney, shi wudda goh a di ᴱfair.
4. Dem wi tek wau ᴱtaxi goh a di ᴱairport ᴱif dem fren noh iyeb'l fi tek dem.
5. Mi aggo ᴱtravel goh a ᴱAsia nex iyer.
6. Di ᴱgroup aggo ᴱtravel ᴱup di riva ᴱby buot.
7. ᴱIt aggo bi wau ᴱnice dyeh ᴱtomorrow bikaah ᴱit aggo bi ᴱsunny.
8. ᴱIf wi noh ak ᴱnow, wi wi ᴱlose di ᴱdeal.
9. ᴱNelly auh ᴱJerome a goh bi inna ᴱSt. Ann ᴱtomorrow.
10. Mi wudda si yuh a di paati.

Practice Exercise 57

Translate the following sentences to English, and underline the verbs in the future or conditional future tense.

1. Mi wudda spen ᴱtime wid mi fren ᴱif shi did ha ᴱtime.

    _____

2. Wi aggo goh pan di ᴱschool ᴱtrip ᴱtomorrow.

    _____

3. Di pyenta aggo pyent di ᴱwall inna di ᴱkitchen ᴱif im ha ᴱenough pyent lef.

    _____

4. ᴱIf yuh noh siim tudeh, yuh noh wi siim ᴱuntil nex ᴱweek.

    _____

117

5. Mi wudda gi yuh disya ᴱbag ya ᴱif mi did ha wau nex ᴱone.

   _____

6. Di ᴱevent aggo bi nex mont.

   _____

7. ᴱHenry an ᴱGeorge aggo hyeh di ᴱresult a di ᴱexam inna ᴱtwo dyeh.

   _____

8. Mi aggo lef fi goh huom ᴱnow.

   _____

9. Dem aggo ᴱfly goh a ᴱTrinidad an den dem aggoᴱ fly goh a ᴱSt. Lucia.

   _____

10. Datdeh pikini deh aggo ᴱcome fos inna di ryes.

    _____

Practice Exercise 58

Fill in the blanks with appropriate verbs in the future or conditional future tense to complete the following sentences.

1. Mi _____ yuh ᴱmoney ᴱif yuh ᴱneed ih.

2. Kenisha _____ ᴶwid ᴶaar fren ᴶfi two week.

3. Aalduo wi noh pyeh fi di ᴱbook ᴱyet, wi _____ ih fi di ᴱclass.

4. ᴱIf ᴱTrisha did syev aar ᴱmoney fi goh a di ᴱzoo, shi _____ iyeb'l fi goh.

5. ᴱJunior _____ im fren ᴱwhen im goh a di ᴱmovie tyeta.

6. Mi _____ yuh wid yuh ᴱassignment ᴱif mi did ha ᴱtime.

7. ^EJerome _____ yuh ^Ewhen im ^Eget im fuon.

8. ^EIf mi madda did ha yaan, shi _____ wau sweta fi aar grandaata.

9. ^EShelly an ^EPeter _____ fi di tes tugedda.

10. Shi _____ yuh wau ^Edress fi ^Ewear.

Practice Exercise 59

Translate the sentences from Practice Exercise 58 to English.

1. _____

2. _____

3. _____

4. _____

5. _____

6. _____

7. _____

8. _____

9. _____

10. _____

Practice Exercise 60

State whether the underlined part of the following sentences is in the future or conditional future tense by writing the tense on the line.

1. Im <u>wudda goh</u> pan di ^Etrip if im did ha ^Etime.

    _____

2. Alecia ^J<u>wi help</u> ^Jyuh out if ^Jyuh ^Jinna trouble.

    _____

3. Dem <u>aggo ^Emov</u>e goh a ^ESt. Catherine ^Eby di en a di mont.

    _____

4. ᴱJack <u>ooh lef</u> ᴱsoon, ᴱbut mi naah goh wid im.

   _____

5. ᴱMarcia ᴱlike fi ᴱdance, soh shi <u>aggo tek</u> ᴱdance ᴱlesson.

   _____

6. Mi faada <u>wi pyent</u> di ᴱchair dem soh dem noh ᴱget ᴱrusty.

   _____

7. ᴱStacy an di adda ᴱstudent dem <u>aggo iht</u> dem ᴱlunch ᴱnow.

   _____

8. Aalduo mi did seh mi <u>a goh</u> ᴱ<u>study</u> tudeh, mi <u>aggo duh</u> it nex ᴱweek.

   _____

9. ᴱIf wi <u>aggo goh</u> a di paak, ᴱthen wi <u>naah goh goh</u> a di maakit.

   _____

10. Di ᴱvase <u>wi bruk</u> ᴱif ih jap aaf a di tyeb'l.

    _____

Practice Exercise 61

Use the following words to form sentences in the future tense of Jamaican Creole. Identify the part of speech of the word you used by writing it on the line (e.g. noun, verb, etc.).

tyeb'l *n.* table   **kuot** *n., v.* coat
ya *adv., n.* here   **pikcha** *n., v.* picture
duh *v.* do   **ha** *v.* have

1. _____

   Part of speech _____

2. _____

   Part of speech _____

3. _____

Part of speech _____

4. _____

Part of speech _____

5. _____

Part of speech _____

6. _____

Part of speech _____

Reading Comprehensions

Reading Comprehension 1

[J]Di School Trip

[E]Every iyer wi [E]class goh pau wau [E]school [E]trip. Laas iyer, wi did goh a [E]Portland. Dis iyer, wi goh a [E]Black Riva inna [E]St. Elizabeth. Di tiicha did aks di pikini dem inna di [E]class weh dem wau fi goh, an nof a wi seh wi wau fi goh a diffrent diffrent plyes. Wi did [E]narrow [E]it dong [E]to chrii plyes an [E]everybody vuot. Muos pikini en [E]up [E]choosing fi goh a [E]Black Riva. A neva deh mi did wau fi goh, [E]but a dehsoh muos a di adda pikini dem did wau fi goh.

Mi neva did [E]excited [E]at fos, [E]but den mi did staat [E]get [E]excited bout di [E]trip. A did di fos [E]time mi a goh a [E]St. Elizabeth, an [E]eventually mi did a [E]look faawod [E]to [E]it. Fi [E]few [E]weeks, wi mek [E]plans bout wa wi aggo duh. Muos a wi seh wi wau fi goh pan wau buot [E]ride pan di Black Riva an den goh a wau [E]local factri fi si [E]how dem mek [E]rum an adda [E]liquor.

Ih did a wau [E]hot dyeh, soh mi tiicha [E]suggest seh wi fi [E]wear [E]light cola cluoz. Mi [E]decide fi [E]dress inna wau [E]white [E]T-shirt an [E]blue [E]jeans [E]pants. Wi [E]all [E]pack [E]up inna wau [E]big [E]bus, an di jraiva [E]head inna di [E]direction a [E]St. Elizabeth. Wi [E]school inna [E]Manchester, soh [E]it did tek wi oova [E]one owa fi [E]reach deh. Wi paak inna wau sumaal paaking ᴱlot, an den wi mek wi wyeh goh a di riva weh ᴱpeople ᴱfrom di buot ᴱtour did a wyet pan wi.

Di ᴱBlack Riva a wau riva weh ᴱthirty-ᴶchrii ᴱmile ᴱlong, an ᴱcrocodile inna di waata. Di fos ᴱcrocodile wi si did ᴱbig an ᴱlong. Ih did deh pan wau ᴱrock nex ᴱto di waata an ᴱlook ᴱlike ᴱit did a ᴱenjoy di ᴱsunshine. Wi si ᴱfew adda ᴱcrocodile ᴱup di riva. Di buot ᴱride did ᴱnice an ᴱrelaxing. ᴱWhen wi ᴱget ᴱback, a did ᴱtime fi ᴱlunch. Afta ᴱlunch, wi ᴱhead ᴱout fi di factri weh mek ᴱliquor.

A di factri, wau ᴱguide tek wi chruu di ᴱfacility an shuo wi di ᴱequipment dem weh dem ᴱuse fi mek ᴱrum. Di ᴱguide dem ᴱmix ᴱmolasses, waata, an ᴱyeast inna wau ᴱbig cantyena. Dem den sepa-ryet di ᴱalcohol frau di ᴱmixture. Di ᴱguide seh dem ᴱput di ᴱalcohol inna wau ᴱbarrel, an den dem iyej ᴱit fi wau ᴱperiod a ᴱtime. Ih did intrestin fi si ᴱhow dem mek ih. ᴱBy di en a di dyeh, wi did taiyad an ᴱready fi goh huom.

1. What is the name of the narrator?
    A. John.
    B. Sabrina.
    C. Kenny.
    D. The writer did not state his or her name.

2. What was the name of the parish the class visited last year?
    A. Black River.
    B. St. Ann.
    C. St. Elizabeth.
    D. Portland.

3. How many destinations did the student choose from?
    A. Three.
    B. Four.
    C. Two.
    D. None.

4. How did the writer feel about the trip to the Black River at first?
    A. Happy.
    B. Dreamy.

C. Unexcited.

D. Excited.

5. What specific word did the writer use to describe the temperature of the day?

A. Sunny.

B. Warm.

C. Cool.

D. Hot.

6. What did the students do on the trip?

A. They learned to make rum and went for a van ride.

B. They learned how syrup is made and went for a boat ride.

C. They went for lunch at a restaurant and went on a boat ride.

D. They went to a factory and went on a boat ride.

7. What did the writer wear on the trip?

A. T-shirt and skirt.

B. White t-shirt and black jeans.

C. Blue t-shirt and white jeans.

D. White t-shirt and blue jeans.

8. Where is the writer's school located?

A. St. Elizabeth.

B. Black River.

C. Manchester.

D. St. Ann.

9. What animals were seen at the Black River?

A. Manatees.

B. Crocodiles.

C. Alligators.

D. Catfish.

10. What did the students see at the factory?

A. Equipment to make vodka.

B. Equipment to make wine.

C. Equipment to make rum.

D. A wine cellar.

Reading Comprehension 2

Natty Mou'n

A did samma inna di ^Ecool, ^Ehilly iyeria weh dem ^Ecall Natty Mou'n. A did di fos samma ^ELetisha a spen deh. ^ELetisha ^Efamily ^Emove goh deh frau di adda ^Eside a di ^Eisland inna ^ESt. Mary. Shi neva did ^Ehappy ^Ewhen dem fos ^Emove goh deh ^Ebecause shi did haffi lef ^Eall a aar fren dem, aar ^Eschool, aar ^Ecommunity, an evriting weh shi eva nuo. Pan tap a dat, a did ^Eright bifuo di ryeni ^Eseason, an bwuay, di ryen kyah ^Efall inna Natty Mou'n. ^EIn ^Efact, di ryeni ^Eseason laas fi ^Eone huol mont.

Afta a ^Efew mont, ^ELetisha ^Eget ^Eused ^Eto ^Eliving inna Natty Mou'n. Shi did staat fi ^Elike ih. Shi mek ^Enew fren, staat wau ^Enew ^Eschool, an shi ^Eget ^Eused ^Eto fi ^Elive ^Eup inna di mou'n. Aar fyevrit paat a ^Eliving inna Natty Mou'n a di ^Eview a di ^Esea frau ^Ehigh ^Eup inna di ^Ehill dem. Inna di maanin, shi cudda si ^Eout ^Eto ^Ewhere di ^Eblue ^Esea ^Emeet di pyel ^Eblue ^Esky. Di iyer ^Eup deh did ^Enice an ^Ecool.

Inna samma, ^ELetisha ^Elike fi ^Ewatch di faama dem ^Epick an ^Ecarry ^Ebreadfruit frau ^Eup inna di ^Ewoods ^Ecome ^Eback a Natty Mou'n. Aar faada an adda ^Epeople inna Natty Mou'n ^Eused ^Eto ^Ebuy di ^Efruit dem frau di faama dem. ^ESometimes wau ^Eman nyem Missa ^EDiggs did ^Edrive wau tracta, an ^ELetisha an aar ^Efamily wudda ^Eride goh a di faam fi ^Ebuy di ^Efruit dem. Dem wudda den ^Eride ^Eback goh a Natty Mou'n inna di tracta wid di ^Ebreadfruit dem.

Missa ^EDiggs den ^Ebuy di ^Ebreadfruit dem frau di faama dem an den goh ^Esell dem ^Eto wau ^Ecompany weh ^Eship di ^Ebreakfruit dem goh a farin. ^EWhen a ^Emango ^Eseason, im wudda ^Ebuy ^Emango tuh. Dat a did ^ELetisha fyevrit ^Etime fi goh wid aar ^Efamily pan di tracta bikaah dem wudda ^Eget fi ^Epick an ^Ecarry huom ^Esome a di ^Emango dem weh di faama dem noh ^Ewant.

1. Where did Letisha's family move to Natty Mou'n from?
   A. Other side of Natty Mou'n.
   B. Port Maria.
   C. St. Mary.
   D. St. Ann.

2. What lasts for a month in Natty Mou'n?
   A. Summer.
   B. Breadfruit season.
   C. Mango season.
   D. Rainy season.

3. Letisha liked the view of _____?
   A. the sea from high up in the mountain.
   B. the river below the mountain.
   C. the breadfruit trees on the mountain.
   D. the sea from the seashore.

4. Summer was a time when the farmers of Natty Mou'n would sell _____?
   A. apples and avocadoes.
   B. star-apples.
   C. guavas and pineapples.
   D. breadfruits and mangoes.

5. Which statement was made by the writer?
   A. Afta a ᴱfew mont, Letisha ᴱget ᴱused ᴱto ᴱliving inna Natty Mou'n.
   B. Letisha did ᴱlove Natty Mou'n ᴱfrom di fos ᴱtime shi goh deh.
   C. Nof ᴱbreadfruit ᴱtree gruo inna Natty Mou'n.
   D. Mr. Diggs did a di richis ᴱman inna Natty Mou'n.

6. What was Letisha's favorite time to go with her family on the tractor?
   A. Summer.
   B. Breadfruit season.
   C. Rainy season.
   D. Mango season.

7. What can you conclude based on the passage?
   A. Breadfruit trees can only grow on mountains.
   B. People from certain foreign countries buy breadfruits.
   C. People who live in foreign countries do not like mangoes.
   D. Missa Diggs only exports breadfruits.

8. In what season did Letisha and her family move to
   Natty Mou'n?
   A. The writer did not say.
   B. Summer.
   C. Winter
   D. The rainy season.

9. How old was Letisha?
   A. Twelve
   B. Eleven
   C. Eight
   D. The writer's age was not mentioned in the passage.

10. What can we determine from the passage?
    A. Only Letisha and her family buy breadfruits from
       the farmers.
    B. Mr. Diggs is a businessman who buys breadfruits and
       mangoes for exportation.
    C. The breadfruit trees are close to Letisha's house.
    D. Letisha only likes mangoes but dislikes breadfruits.

Reading Comprehension 3

Wau Dyeh A Di ᴱZoo

Mi did a ᴱsix iyer uol di fos ᴱtime mi goh a di ᴱzoo. Mi uolda coz'n
dem did goh deh di iyer bifuo, an dem did seh dem ha nof ᴱfun, soh
mi did wau fi goh. Mi ᴱbeg mi madda an mi faada fi nof ᴱmonths fi tek
mi dyer. Wi did lef wi yaad ᴱearly inna di maanin bifuo nof ᴱtraffic
deh pan di ruod. ᴱWhen wi ᴱreach di ᴱzoo, di paakin ᴱlot did aalmuos
ᴱempty, an wi cudda paak cluos ᴱto di ᴱfront gyet soh wi neva haffi
ᴱwalk ᴱtoo ᴱfar.

Di fos plyes wi goh a did di ᴱmonkey encluosment. Wi si aal diffrent
ᴱtype a ᴱmonkey. Wi si wau ᴱgroup a ᴱfive ᴱBlack ᴱFace ᴱmonkey. Dem
did a ᴱswing frau ᴱbranch ᴱto ᴱbranch, an dem did a ᴱlook pan wi wid
ᴱcuriousity. Wi den si ᴱsome ᴱGolden ᴱLion ᴱTamarin ᴱMonkey wid

dem ^{E}red ^{E}fur, ^{E}some ^{E}Spider ^{E}Monkey, an ^{E}some ^{E}Squirrel ^{E}Monkey. Mi an mi madda did tek a ^{E}few ^{E}selfie ^{E}in ^{E}front a di kyej dem.

Wi ^{E}move ^{E}on ^{E}to di ^{E}lion encluosment. ^{E}Two ^{E}lion did inna wau laaj iyeria; ^{E}one myel an ^{E}one fiimyel. Dem ^{E}roar ^{E}when dem si wi a ^{E}come. ^{E}One a di ^{E}lion dem staat ^{E}walk ^{E}back an fout ^{E}inside di encluosment. Di adda ^{E}one ^{E}lie dong pan di groun an ^{E}look ^{E}like ih did a ^{E}sleep. ^{E}Daddy did muo ^{E}excited fi tek ^{E}picture ^{E}in ^{E}front a di ^{E}lion encluosment dan ^{E}in ^{E}front a di ^{E}monkey encluosment.

Wi den si sinyek, ^{E}bear, ^{E}penquin, ^{E}cheetah, an ^{E}crocodile. Nof ^{E}people did deh a di ^{E}zoo, an mi si nof adda pikini a ^{E}walk roun wid dem ^{E}family. Afta di huol ^{E}heap a ^{E}walking aroun, wi did ^{E}get taiyad an ^{E}hungry. Mi did ^{E}glad fi tek a bryek an iht ^{E}some ^{E}lunch. Afta ^{E}lunch, wi ^{E}visit di ^{E}gorilla encluosment. Wi si sooh ^{E}exotic ^{E}birds, sooh ^{E}ostrich, ^{E}zebra, an ^{E}hippopotamus. Afta wi si di ^{E}hippopotamus dem, wi lef. Mi did a ^{E}look faawod fi ^{E}tell mi fren ^{E}Alain bout di ^{E}experience di nex dyeh.

1. Why did the writer wish to go to the zoo?
   A. They opened a new enclosement with penquins.
   B. It was summer, and the weather was warm.
   C. Her cousins went last year and had a lot of fun.
   D. She had gone to the zoo before, and it was fun.

2. How did the family get to the zoo?
   A. They took the bus.
   B. They took the train.
   C. They drove their own vehicle.
   D. In a relative's vehicle.

3. The family parked their vehicle
   A. close to the back gate.
   B. close to the front gate.
   C. next to the main entrance.
   D. way in the back.

4. The first place the family went to was
   A. the monkey enclosement.
   B. a restaurant.

    C. the lion enclosement.

    D. to see the tigers.

5. At what place did the writer first take a photo?

    A. The monkey enclosement.

    B. A restaurant.

    C. The lion enclosement.

    D. The tiger enlosement.

6. What animals roared when the family approached?

    A. The jaguars.

    B. The tigers.

    C. The gorillas.

    D. The lions.

7. What place was the writer's father most excited to take a picture in front of?

    A. Tiger enclosement.

    B. Jaguar enclosement.

    C. Cheetah enclosement.

    D. Lion enclosement.

8. According to the passage, there were _____ people at the zoo.

    A. few.

    B. some.

    C. many.

    D. too many.

9. The family left the zoo after

    A. 1pm.

    B. they saw the peacocks.

    C. they saw the hippopotamus.

    D. they started to feel tired.

10. What was the name of the writer's friend?

    A. Alisa.

    B. Alain

    C. Alan

    D. Areta.

Reading Comprehension 4

How ᴶFi Write ᴶWau Essay

Yuh ha nof diffrent ᴱtype a ᴱessay, an di wyeh yuh ᴱdevelop yuh pyepa dipen pan di ᴱtype a ᴱessay weh yuh a ᴱwrite. ᴱGenerally duo, yuh ha sooh tings weh yuh kyah duh fi mek ᴱsure yuh ᴱwrite wau ᴱgood ᴱessay. Yuh wau fi gyadda infamyeshan frau nof ᴱdiffrent ᴱsource an ᴱput ᴱit tugedda ᴱinna wau wyeh weh adda ᴱpeople kyah andastan.

Di fos ting yuh kyah duh a ᴱread adda ᴱpeople ᴱessay an si ᴱhow dem aaganaiz dem pyepa. Dis wi gi yuh wau ᴱidea bout ᴱhow fi aaganaiz fi yuh. Mek ᴱsure seh a ᴱpeople ᴱwho ᴱknowledgeable bout di ᴱtopic weh dem a ᴱwrite bout. Yuh wi si ᴱhow dem ᴱdevelop an soppuot di ᴱpoint dem weh dem mek inna di ᴱessay.

Di sekan ting fi duh a fi ᴱread nof ᴱbook pan di ᴱtopic weh yuh a ᴱwrite bout. Yuh kyah goh a yuh ᴱlocal laibri an fain di ᴱbook dem wid di ᴱtopic weh yuh ᴱneed. Yuh kyah ᴱlook fi ᴱjournal ᴱarticle, newsⱼpyepa ᴱarticle, an adda ᴱwritten ᴱsource a infamyeshan pan di ᴱtopic weh yuh a ᴱresearch. Yuh kyah ᴱalso ᴱuse di intanet fi fain infamyeshan. Mek ᴱsure fi kip a lis a di ᴱsource dem weh yuh ᴱuse soh yuh kyah gi ᴱcredit ᴱto dem. Aaganaiz di infamyeshan inna wau faamat weh adda ᴱpeople kyah falla.

Di tûrd ting weh yuh kyah duh a fi ᴱtalk ᴱto ᴱpeople ᴱwho nuo bout di ᴱtopic. Yuh kyah ᴱtalk ᴱto yuh tiicha dem an fain ᴱout wa dem expek frau yuh. Aks dem fi lis ᴱall a di ᴱelement dem weh yuh fi ᴱhave inna di ᴱessay an di faamat weh di ᴱessay fi falla. Uolda ᴱpeople ha nof ᴱexperience, soh yuh kyah ᴱtalk ᴱto yuh uolda ᴱrelative dem an si ᴱif dem kyah ᴱprovide yuh wid infamyeshan.

ᴱFinally, yuh kyah ᴱwrite yuh ᴱessay an aks summadi fi ᴱread ᴱit an gi yuh ᴱfeedback. Aks di ᴱperson fi ᴱspot ᴱgrammatical ᴱerror an gi ᴱfeedback pan di tings dem weh dem tink yuh kyah ᴱimprove pan. ᴱRead chruu yuh ᴱessay wau ᴱfew ᴱtimes ᴱuntil yuh ᴱfeel ᴱconfident seh di ᴱsentence dem soun ᴱgood tugedda an yuh ᴱessay ᴱfree frau ᴱerror.

1. What can be concluded from the passage?
    A. Some people love to write but most people do not.

B. There was no mention of people liking or disliking writing.

C. Some people dislike writing, and some people do not.

D. A lot of people love to write, and a lot of people do not.

2. The aim of the passage was to
   A. explain how to write an essay.
   B. explain how to be a better writer.
   C. explain how to write a story.
   D. explain how to write a book.

3. What was the second strategy the writer identified?
   A. Reading plenty of books on the topic that you are writing about.
   B. Asking someone to edit your work.
   C. Reading random books.
   D. Asking your parents to edit your essay.

4. How many strategies did the writer identify?
   A. Five.
   B. Three.
   C. Four.
   D. One.

5. Which of the following statements was made in the passage?
   A. You should read through your essay to make sure it sounds good and is free from errors.
   B. Reading and correcting your essay is important if writing a formal essay.
   C. You need at least three sources to write a good essay.
   D. Essays are difficult to edit when they are long.

6. What are some places to find information according to the passage?
   A. People you know.
   B. Your local bookstore.
   C. Books and the internet.
   D. Books, newspaper articles, journal articles, the internet, and older relatives.

7. What list is important to keep when writing an essay?
    A. List in your journal.
    B. List of sources you used to write the essay.
    C. List of book sources.
    D. All sources, even if you did not use them.

8. What types of essays did the writer identify?
    A. The writer did not identify any.
    B. Expository and persuasive.
    C. Argumentative and expository.
    D. Persuasive and argumentative.

9. What statement did the writer make?
    A. Your essay is a collection of your thoughts.
    B. You should write only esssays on topics that you are interested in.
    C. Essays are difficult to write, so most people do not like to write them.
    D. You should organize your essay in a format that other people can follow.

10. One thing that other people can give to make your essay better is
    A. feedback on your essay.
    B. a lecture by your parents.
    C. a book.
    D. talking to them.

Frequently Used Jamaican Proverbs

The following proverbs are commonly used in Jamaica Creole. As with English proverbs, the syntax of proverbs in Jamaican Creole is not necessarily used in everyday conversation. However, proverbs are frequently thrown in to express complex ideas with simple words. Words in parenthesis are inserted for better understanding of the proverb.

Jamaican Proverb	Translation
Anno syem dyeh ᴱleaf jap inna waata ih ra'n.	It is not same day [that] leaf drops in water it [will] rot.
ᴱBad ᴱluck wos dau obya.	Bad luck [is] worse than obeah. (*Obeah is a belief system that involves rituals and curses, much like witchcraft and voodoo.*)
Chicken merry, hawk deh ᴶnear.	Chicken [is] merry, [but] hawk is near.
ᴱCockroach noh bizniz inna ᴱfowl ᴱfight.	Cockroach [has] no business in fowl fight.
Cowad ᴱman kip soun buon.	[a] Coward man keeps sound bones.
Doppi nuo ᴱwho fi frai'n.	[a] Ghost knows who to frighten.
ᴱEvery mikk'l mek a mokk'l.	Every bit makes a lot.

Jamaican Proverb	Translation
Fos ^Elaugh anno ^Elaugh.	First laugh is not laugh.
	(*Its always best to have the last laugh.*)
^EFowl weh ^Efeed a yaad ^Eeasy fi ketch.	Fowl that feeds at [a] home is easy to catch.
^EHag seh di fos waata yuh si, yuh ^Ewash.	Hog says the first water you see, you wash.
^EHungry mek puss nyam paach caan.	Hunger makes puss eat parched corn.
^EIf ^Efish weh goh a riva ^Ebottom ^Etell yuh seh shaak dong deh, ^Ebelieve ih.	If fish that goes to river bottom tells you that shark is down there, believe it.
^EIf yuh wau ^Egood, yuh nuoz haffi ^Erun.	If you want good, your nose has to run.
	(*If you want to achieve, you have to work hard.*)
Mi chuo mi caan; mi noh ^Ecall noh ^Efowl.	I threw my corn; I didn't call any fowls.
Noh chob'l chob'l ^Etill chob'l chob'l yuh.	Don't trouble trouble until trouble troubles you.
One, one ^Jcuoco, full ^Jbaaskit.	One, one cocoa, full basket.
	(*Each cocoa helps to fill a basket.*)
^EPuss auh daag noh ha di syem ^Eluck.	Puss and dog do not have the same luck.
Wa noh ^Edead, noh dashweh.	What is not dead, don't throw away.
Wa noh ^Ekill, fah'n; wa noh fah'n figah'n.	What doesn't kill, fattens; what doesn't fatten [is] forgotten.
Weh ih maaga, a deh ih pap.	Where it is slim, it is there it breaks.
^EWho kyaah hyeh aggo ^Efeel; finga mash, noh badda ^Ecry.	Who cannot hear will feel; finger mashed, don't bother [to] cry.
	(*If you refuse to listen to reason, you will suffer the consequences.*)

Appendix

Tenses of Jamaican Creole Verbs

Verbs	Present Tense
aada *order*	aada
aks *ask*	aks
ansa *answer*	ansa
baak *bark*	baak
barro *borrow*	barro
bi *be*	a; deh; bi
brok *break*	brok
byed *bathe*	byed
chaaj *charge*	chaaj
chaka-chaka *mess up*	chaka-chaka
chrech *stretch*	chrech
chuo *throw*	chuo
dash-weh *throw away*	dash-weh
distraah *destroy*	distraah
duh *do*	duh
enta *enter*	enta
expek *expect*	expek

Verbs	Present Tense
faam *farm*	faam
figet *forget*	figet
fren-op *make up with; make oneself friendly to*	fren-op
gi *give*	gi
goh *go*	goh
ha *have*	ha
hag-op *handle roughly; speak harshly to*	hag-op
hoks *hack; husk*	hoks
infek *infect*	infek
iyem *aim*	iyem
jaah *draw; pull*	jaah
juk *prick*	juk
ketch *catch*	ketch
konk *hit with sharp blow*	konk
laas *lose*	laas
laba *talk excessively*	laba
lef *leave*	lef
maach *march*	maach
myel *mail*	myel
nyem *name*	nyem
opin *open*	opin
palaav *occupy (something) as if one owns it*	palaav
pudong *put down*	pudong
qwaaril *quarrel*	qwaaril
ryet *rate*	ryet
saach *search*	saach
shub *shove*	shub

Verbs	Present Tense
sidong *sit; sit down*	sidong
suolla *swallow*	suolla
tan-op *stand; stand up*	tan-op
tomp *punch*	tomp
uon *own*	uon
vuot *vote*	vuot
wain *rotate hips*	wain

Verbs	Present Continuous Tense
aada *order*	a aada; aada-in
aks *ask*	a aks; aks-in
ansa *answer*	a ansa; ansa-in
baak *bark*	a baak; baak-in
barro *borrow*	a barro; barro-in
bi *be*	a bi; deh bi; E. being
brok *break*	a brok; brok-in
byed *bathe*	a byed; byed-in
chaaj *charge*	a chaaj; chaaj-in
chaka-chaka *mess up*	a chaka-chaka; chaka-chaka-in
chrech *stretch*	a chrech; chrech-in
chuo *throw*	a chuo; chuo-in
dash-weh *throw away*	a dash-weh; dash-weh-in
distraah *destroy*	a distraah; distraah-in
duh *do*	a duh; duh-in
enta *enter*	a enta; enta-in
expek *expect*	a expek; expect-in
faam *farm*	a faam; faam-in
figet *forget*	a figet; figet-in

Verbs	Present Continuous Tense
fren-op *make up with; make oneself friendly to*	a fren-op
gi *give*	a gi; gi-in; E. giving
goh *go*	a goh; goh-in
ha *have*	a ha; E. having
hag-op *handle roughly; speak harshly to*	a hag-op; hag-op-in
hoks *hack; husk*	a hoks; hoks-in
infek *infect*	a infek; infek-in
iyem *aim*	a iyem; iyem-in
jaah *draw; pull*	a jaah; jaah-in
juk *prick*	a juk; juk-in
ketch *catch*	a ketch; ketch-in
konk *hit with sharp blow*	a konk; konk-in
laas *lose*	a laas; laas-in
laba *talk excessively*	a laba; laba-in
lef *leave*	a lef; lef-in
maach *march*	a maach; maach-in
myel *mail*	a myel; myel-in
nyem *name*	a nyem; nyem-in
opin *open*	a opin; opin-in
palaav *occupy (something) as if one owns it*	a palaav; palaav-in
pudong *put down*	a pudong; pudong-in
qwaaril *quarrel*	a qwaaril; qwaaril-in
ryet *rate*	a ryet; ryet-in
saach *search*	a saach; saach-in
shub *shove*	a shub; shub-in
sidong *sit; sit down*	sidong; sidong-in
suolla *swallow*	a suolla; suolla-in

Verbs	Present Continuous Tense
tan-op *stand; stand up*	tan-op; tan-op-in
tomp *punch*	a tomp; tomp-in
uon *own*	a uon; uon-in
vuot *vote*	a vuot; vuot-in
wain *rotate hips*	a wain; wain-in

Verbs	Simple Past Tense

(Note that *did* is sometimes replaced with *beeh, weeh, beeh did,* or *weeh did,* e.g., *beeh aada, weeh aada, beeh did aada,* or *weeh did aada.* The verb *bi* is addressed separately. All the conjugations for the verb *bi* are outlined below.)

aada *order*	did aada; aada
aks *ask*	did aks; aks
ansa *ansa*	did ansa; ansa
baak *bark*	did baak; baak
barro *borrow*	did barro; barro
bi *be*	did a (a did; ben a; wen a; beeh did a; weeh did a); did deh (beeh deh; weeh deh; beeh did deh; weeh did deh); did bi (beeh bi; weeh bi; beeh did bi; weeh did bi)
brok *break*	did brok; brok
byed *bathe*	did byed; byed
chaaj *charge*	did chaaj; chaaj
chaka-chaka *mess up*	did chaka-chaka; chaka-chaka
chrech *stretch*	did chrech; chrech
chuo *throw*	did chuo; chuo
dash-weh *throw away*	did dash-weh; dash-weh
distraah *destroy*	did distraah; distraah
duh *do*	did duh; duh

Verbs	Simple Past Tense
enta *enter*	did enta; enta
expek *expect*	did expek; expek
faam *farm*	did faam; faam
figet *forget*	did figet; figet
fren-op *make up with; make oneself friendly to*	did fren-op; fren-op
gi *give*	did gi; gi
goh *go*	did goh; goh
ha *have*	did ha; ha
hag-op *handle roughly; speak harshly to*	did hag-op; hag-og
hoks *hack; husk*	did hoks; hoks
infek *infect*	did infek; infek
iyem *aim*	did iyem; iyem
jaah *draw; pull*	did jaah; jaah
juk *prick*	did juk; juk
ketch *catch*	did ketch; ketch
konk *hit with sharp blow*	did konk; konk
laas *lose*	did laas; laas
laba *talk excessively*	did laba; laba
lef *leave*	did lef; lef
maach *march*	did maach; maach
myel *mail*	did myel; myel
nyem *name*	did nyem; nyem
opin *open*	did opin; opin
palaav *occupy (something) as if one owns it*	did palaav; palaav
pudong *put down*	did pudong; pudong
qwaaril *quarrel*	did qwaaril; qwaaril
ryet *rate*	did ryet; ryet

Verbs	Simple Past Tense
saach *search*	did saach; saach
shub *shove*	did shub; shub
sidong *sit; sit down*	did sidong; sidong
suolla *swallow*	did suolla; suolla
tan-op *stand; stand up*	did tan-op; tan-op
tomp *punch*	did tomp; tomp
uon *own*	did uon; uon
vuot *vote*	did vuot; vuot
wain *rotate hips*	did wain; wain

Verbs	Continuous Past/Continuous Past Perfect Tense

(Note that *did a* is sometimes replaced with *ben a, wen a, did deh, beeh deh, weeh deh, beeh did deh,* or *weeh did deh,* e.g., *ben a aada, wen a aada, beeh deh aada, weeh deh aada, beeh did deh aada,* or *weeh did deh aada. Sidong* and *tan-op* are exceptions. Their conjugations are outlined below.)

aada *order*	did a aada
aks *ask*	did a aks
ansa *ansa*	did a ansa
baak *bark*	did a baak
barro *borrow*	did a barro
bi *be*	did a bi
brok *break*	did a brok
byed *bathe*	did a byed
chaaj *charge*	did a chaaj
chaka-chaka *mess up*	did a chaka-chaka
chrech *stretch*	did a chrech
chuo *throw*	did a chuo

Verbs	Continuous Past/Continuous Past Perfect Tense
dash-weh *throw away*	did a dash-weh
distraah *destroy*	did a distraah
duh *do*	did a duh
enta *enter*	did a enta
expek *expect*	did a expek
faam *farm*	did a faam
figet *forget*	did a figet
fren-op *make up with; make oneself friendly to*	did a fren-op
gi *give*	did a gi
goh *go*	did a goh
ha *have*	did a ha
hag-op *handle roughly; speak harshly to*	did a hag-op
hoks *hack; husk*	did a hoks
infek *infect*	did a infek
iyem *aim*	did a iyem
jaah *draw; pull*	did a jaah
juk *prick*	did a juk
ketch *catch*	did a ketch
konk *hit with sharp blow*	did a konk
laas *lose*	did a laas
laba *talk excessively*	did a laba
lef *leave*	did a lef
maach *march*	did a maach
myel *mail*	did a myel
nyem *name*	did a nyem
opin *open*	did a opin

Verbs	Continuous Past/Continuous Past Perfect Tense
palaav *occupy (something) as if one owns it*	did a palaav
pudong *put down*	did a pudong
qwaaril *quarrel*	did a qwaaril
ryet *rate*	did a ryet
saach *search*	did a saach
shub *shove*	did a shub
sidong *sit; sit down*	did sidong; beeh sidong; weeh sidong; beeh did sidong; weeh did sidong
suolla *swallow*	did a suolla
tan-op *stand; stand up*	did tan-op; beeh tan-op; weeh tan-op; beeh did tan-op; weeh did tan-op
tomp *punch*	did a tomp
uon *own*	did a uon
vuot *vote*	did a vuot
wain *rotate hips*	did a wain

Verbs	Present Perfect Tense
aada *order*	aada
aks *ask*	aks
ansa *answer*	ansa
baak *bark*	baak
barro *borrow*	barro
bi *be*	a; deh; E. been
brok *break*	brok
byed *bathe*	byed

Verbs	Present Perfect Tense
chaaj *charge*	chaaj
chaka-chaka *mess up*	chaka-chaka
chrech *stretch*	chrech
chuo *throw*	chuo
dash-weh *throw away*	dash-weh
distraah *destroy*	distraah
duh *do*	duh; E. done
enta *enter*	enta
expek *expect*	expek
faam *farm*	faam
figet *forget*	figet
fren-op *make up with; make oneself friendly to*	fren-op
gi *give*	gi
goh *go*	E. gone
ha *have*	ha
hag-op *handle roughly; speak harshly to*	hag-op
hoks *hack; husk*	hoks
infek *infect*	infek
iyem *aim*	iyem
jaah *draw; pull*	jaah
juk *prick*	juk
ketch *catch*	ketch
konk *hit with sharp blow*	konk
laas *lose*	laas
laba *talk excesively*	laba
lef *leave*	lef
maach *march*	maach
myel *mail*	myel

Verbs	Present Perfect Tense
nyem *name*	nyem
opin *open*	opin
palaav *occupy (something) as if one owns it*	palaav
pudong *put down*	pudong
qwaaril *quarrel*	qwaaril
ryet *rate*	ryet
saach *search*	saach
sidong *sit; sit down*	sidong
shub *shove*	shub
suolla *swallow*	suolla
tan-op *stand; stand up*	tan-op
tomp *punch*	tomp
uon *own*	uon
vuot *vote*	vuot
wain *rotate hips*	wain

Verbs	Past Perfect Tense

(Note that *did* is sometimes replaced with *beeh, weeh, beeh did,* or *weeh did,* e.g., *beeh aada, weeh aada, beeh did aada,* or *weeh did aada.* The verb *bi* is addressed separately. All the conjugations for the verb *bi* are outlined below.)

aada *order*	did aada
aks *ask*	did aks
ansa *answer*	did ansa
baak *bark*	did baak
barro *borrow*	did barro

Verbs	Past Perfect Tense
bi *be*	did a (a did; ben a; wen a; beeh did a; weeh did a); did deh (beeh deh; weeh deh; beeh did deh; weeh did deh); did bi (beeh bi; weeh bi; beeh did bi; weeh did bi)
brok *break*	did brok
byed *bathe*	did byed
chaaj *charge*	did chaaj
chaka-chaka *mess up*	did chaka-chaka
chrech *stretch*	did chrech
chuo *throw*	did chuo
dash-weh *throw away*	did dash-weh
distraah *destroy*	did distraah
duh *do*	did duh
enta *enter*	did enta
expek *expect*	did expek
faam *farm*	did faam
figet *forget*	did figet
fren-op *make up with; make oneself friendly to*	did fren-op
gi *give*	did gi
goh *go*	did goh; E. did gone
ha *have*	did ha
hag-op *handle roughly; speak harshly to*	did hag-op
hoks *hack; husk*	did hoks
infek *infect*	did infek
iyem *aim*	did iyem
jaah *draw; pull*	did jaah
juk *prick*	did juk
ketch *catch*	did ketch

Verbs	Past Perfect Tense
konk *hit with sharp blow*	did konk
laas *lose*	did laas
laba *talk excesively*	did laba
lef *leave*	did lef
maach *march*	did maach
myel *mail*	did myel
nyem *name*	did nyem
opin *open*	did opin
palaav *occupy (something) as if one owns it*	did palaav
pudong *put down*	did pudong
qwaaril *quarrel*	did qwaaril
ryet *rate*	did ryet
saach *search*	did saach
sidong *sit; sit down*	did sidong
shub *shove*	did shub
suolla *swallow*	did suolla
tan-op *stand; stand up*	did tan-op
tomp *punch*	did tomp
uon *own*	did uon
vuot *vote*	did vuot
wain *rotate hips*	did wain

Verbs	Continuous Present Perfect Tense
aada *order*	aada; E. been aada-in
aks *ask*	aks; E. been aks-in
ansa *answer*	ansa; E. been ansa-in

Verbs	Continuous Present Perfect Tense
baak *bark*	baak; E. been baak-in
barro *borrow*	barro; E. been barro-in
bi *be*	a; deh; E. been
brok *break*	brok; E. been brok-in
byed *bathe*	byed; E. been byed-in
chaaj *charge*	chaaj; E. been chaaj-in
chaka-chaka *mess up*	chaka-chaka; E. been chaka-chaka-in
chrech *stretch*	chrech; E. been chrech-in
chuo *throw*	chuo; E. been chuo-in
dash-weh *throw away*	dash-weh; E. been dash-weh-in
distraah *destroy*	distraah; E. been distraah-in
duh *do*	duh; done; E. been doing
enta *enter*	enta; E. been enta-in
expek *expect*	expek; E. been expek-in
faam *farm*	faam; E. been faam-in
figet *forget*	figet; E. been figet-in
fren-op *make up with; make oneself friendly to*	fren-op; E. been fren-op-in
gi *give*	gi; E. been gi-in; E. been giving
goh *go*	E. gone; E. been goh-in
ha *have*	ha; E. been having
hag-op *handle roughly; speak harshly to*	hag-op; E. been hag-op-in
hoks *hack; husk*	hoks; E. been hoks-in
infek *infect*	infek; E. been infek-in
iyem *aim*	iyem; E. been iyem-in
jaah *draw; pull*	jaah; E. been jaah-in
juk *prick*	juk; E. been juk-in

Verbs	Continuous Present Perfect Tense
ketch *catch*	ketch; E. been ketch-in
konk *hit with sharp blow*	konk; E. been konk-in
laas *lose*	laas; E. been laas-in
laba *talk excesively*	laba; E. been laba-in
lef *leave*	lef; E. been lef-in
maach *march*	maach; E. been maach-in
myel *mail*	myel; E. been myel-in
nyem *name*	nyem; E. been nyem-in
opin *open*	opin; E. been opin-in
palaav *occupy (something) as if one owns it*	palaav; E. been palaav-in
pudong *put down*	pudong; E. been pudong-in
qwaaril *quarrel*	qwaaril; E. been qwaaril-in
ryet *rate*	ryet; E. been ryet-in
saach *search*	saach; E. been saach-in
sidong *sit; sit down*	sidong; E. been sidong-in
shub *shove*	shub; E. been shub-in
suolla *swallow*	suolla; E. been suolla-in
tan-op *stand; stand up*	tan-op; E. been tan-op-in
tomp *punch*	tomp; E. been tomp-in
uon *own*	uon; E. been uon-in
vuot *vote*	vuot; E. been vuot-in
wain *rotate hips*	wain; E. been wain-in

Verbs	Future Tense
aada *order*	aggo aada; gweeh aada
aks *ask*	aggo aks; gweeh aks

Verbs	Future Tense
ansa *answer*	aggo ansa; gweeh ansa
baak *bark*	aggo baak; gweeh baak
barro *borrow*	aggo barro; gweeh barro
bi *be*	aggo bi; gweeh bi; aggo deh; gweeh deh
brok *break*	aggo brok; gweeh brok
byed *bathe*	aggo byed; gweeh byed
chaaj *charge*	aggo chaaj; gweeh chaaj
chaka-chaka *mess up*	aggo chaka-chaka gweeh chaka- chaka
chrech *stretch*	aggo chrech; gweeh chrech
chuo *throw*	aggo chuo; gweeh chuo
dash-weh *throw away*	aggo dash-weh; gweeh dash-weh
distraah *destroy*	aggo distraah; gweeh distraah
duh *do*	aggo duh; gweeh duh
enta *enter*	aggo enta; gweeh enta
expek *expect*	aggo expek; gweeh expek
faam *farm*	aggo faam; gweeh faam
figet *forget*	aggo figet; gweeh figet
fren-op *make up with; make oneself friendly to*	aggo fren-op; gweeh fren-op
gi *give*	aggo gi; gweeh gi
goh *go*	aggo goh; gweeh goh
ha *have*	aggo ha; gweeh ha
hag-op *handle roughly; speak harshly to*	aggo hag-op; gweeh hag-op
hoks *hack; husk*	aggo hoks; gweeh hoks
infek *infect*	aggo infek; gweeh infek
iyem *aim*	aggo iyem; gweeh iyem
jaah *draw; pull*	aggo jaah; gweeh jaah

Verbs	Future Tense
juk *prick*	aggo juk; gweeh juk
ketch *catch*	aggo ketch; gweeh ketch
konk *hit with sharp blow*	aggo konk; gweeh konk
laas *lose*	aggo laas; gweeh laas
laba *talk excessively*	aggo laba; gweeh laba
lef *leave*	aggo lef; gweeh lef
maach *march*	aggo maach; gweeh maach
myel *mail*	aggo myel; gweeh myel
nyem *name*	aggo nyem; gweeh nyem
opin *open*	aggo opin; gweeh opin
palaav *occupy (something) as if one owns it*	aggo palaav; gweeh palaav
pudong *put down*	aggo pudong; gweeh pudong
qwaaril *quarrel*	aggo qwaaril; gweeh qwaaril
ryet *rate*	aggo ryet; gweeh ryet
saach *search*	aggo saach; gweeh saach
shub *shove*	aggo shub; gweeh shub
sidong *sit; sit down*	aggo sidong; gweeh sidong
suolla *swallow*	aggo suolla; gweeh suolla
tan-op *stand; stand up*	aggo tan-op; gweeh tan-op
tomp *punch*	aggo tomp; gweeh tomp
uon *own*	aggo uon; gweeh uon
vuot *vote*	aggo vuot; gweeh vuot
wain *rotate hips*	aggo wain; gweeh wain

Verbs	Conditional Future Tense
aada *order*	wi aada; wudda aada
aks *ask*	wi aks; wudda aks

Verbs	Conditional Future Tense
ansa *answer*	wi ansa; wudda ansa
baak *bark*	wi baak; wudda baak
barro *borrow*	wi barro; wudda barro
bi *be*	wi bi; wudda bi; wi deh; wudda deh
brok *break*	wi brok; wudda brok
byed *bathe*	wi byed; wudda byed
chaaj *charge*	wi chaaj; wudda chaaj
chaka-chaka *mess up*	wi chaka-chaka; wudda chaka- chaka
chrech *stretch*	wi chech; wudda chrech
chuo *throw*	wi chuo; wudda chuo
dash-weh *throw away*	wi dash-weh; wudda dash-weh
distraah *destroy*	wi distraah; wudda distraah
duh *do*	wi duh; wudda duh
enta *enter*	wi enta; wudda enta
expek *expect*	wi expek; wudda expek
faam *farm*	wi faam; wudda faam
figet *forget*	wi figet; wudda figet
fren-op *make up with; make oneself friendly to*	wi fren-op; wudda fren-op
gi *give*	wi gi; wudda gi
goh *go*	wi goh; wudda goh
ha *have*	wi ha; wudda ha
hag-op *handle roughly; speak harshly to*	wi hag-op; wudda hag-op
hoks *hack; husk*	wi hoks; wudda hoks
infek *infect*	wi infek; wudda infek
iyem *aim*	wi iyem; wudda iyem
jaah *draw; pull*	wi jaah; wudda jaah

Verbs	Conditional Future Tense
juk *prick*	wi juk; wudda juk
ketch *catch*	wi ketch; wudda ketch
konk *hit with sharp blow*	wi konk; wudda konk
laas *lose*	wi laas; wudda laas
laba *talk excessively*	wi laba; wudda laba
lef *leave*	wi lef; wudda lef
maach *march*	wi maach; wudda maach
myel *mail*	wi myel; wudda myel
nyem *name*	wi nyem; wudda nyem
opin *open*	wi opin; wudda opin
palaav *occupy (something) as if one owns it*	wi palaav; wudda palaav
pudong *put down*	wi pudong; wudda pudong
qwaaril *quarrel*	wi qwaaril; wudda qwaaril
ryet *rate*	wi ryet; wudda ryet
saach *search*	wi saach; wudda saach
shub *shove*	wi shub; wudda shub
sidong *sit; sit down*	wi sidong; wudda sidong
suolla *swallow*	wi suolla; wudda suolla
tan-op *stand; stand up*	wi tan-op; wudda tan-op
tomp *punch*	wi tomp; wudda tomp
uon *own*	wi uon; wudda uon
vuot *vote*	wi vuot; wudda vuot
wain *rotate hips*	wi wain; wudda wain

About the Author

The author was born and grew up in the hills of Clarendon in Jamaica. She is also the author of *Jamaican Creole Grammar* and *Speak Jamaican: A Guide To Fluency.* She works in the field of psychology, but writing has remained one of her greatest passions. The author has the desire to see Jamaican Creole legitimized as a language. She hopes that this book will aid in that process